NEAL-SCHUMAN

Authoritative Guide to Web Search Engines

SUSAN MAZE, DAVID MOXLEY, AND DONNA J. SMITH

NEAL-SCHUMAN NETGUIDE SERIES

NEAL-SCHUMAN PUBLISHERS, INC.
NEW YORK   LONDON

Published by Neal-Schuman Publishers, Inc.
100 Varick Street
New York, NY 10013

Printed and bound in the United States of America.

Library of Congress Cataloging-in-Publication Data
Maze, Susan.
  Neal-Schuman authoritative guide to Web search engines / Susan Maze,
David Moxley, and Donna J. Smith.
      p.   cm.—(Neal-Schuman net-guide series)
  Includes bibliographical references and index.
  ISBN 1–55570–305–4
  1. World Web Web (information retrieval system) 2. Database
searching—Computer programs. I. Moxley, David. II. Smith, Donna J.
III. Title. IV. Series.
TK5105.882.M39   1997
025.04—DC21   97–14805

Contents

**SECTION III:
UNDERSTANDING AND USING SEVEN SEARCH ENGINES**

SECTION IV:
WEB SEARCH TOOLS IN CONTEXT

Acknowledgments

We would like to thank the faculty, staff, and students of the School of Library and Informational Sciences at the University of Missouri - Columbia (especially Dr. Mary Ellen Sievert) for providing a rich environment for learning and discussing Web retrieval; Glenn Kuhlman for his assistance with the graphics in the book; and our understanding families (especially Melanie Johnson-Moxley for the index and Jordan Maze for not running away).

Preface

With few exceptions, most everything written about specific Web search engines thus far has consisted of reiterations of promotional materials and FAQ (Frequently Asked Questions) lists taken from the search tools themselves.

The *Neal-Schuman Authoritative Guide to Web Search Engines* presents the results of thousands of hours spent studying how Web search engines actually gather, store, and retrieve information, as well as assesses many issues surrounding effective retrieval.

One of the most surprising findings reported here is that although Web search tools often appear to be quite sophisticated and complex, they are actually remarkably simple. This is *not* to say that they are simple to use well, but rather that none of them do as much as Web searchers tend to think they do. Not one of them searches or indexes the entire Web—or even comes close to it. None of them achieve the flexibility and power of traditional commercial database vendors like Dialog. Unlike a library catalog, no search engine provides or utilizes a controlled vocabulary or an authority file to standardize access to information sources. In fact, this *Guide* shows that—by and large—Web search engines are the result and embodiment of ongoing automated processes designed to perform "quick and dirty" collecting and indexing of Web pages.

The success—and popularity—of these tools lies largely in the fact that they operate in an environment, the Web, so rich with raw data that through sheer brute strength efforts they can create databases large enough to retrieve *something* for almost any search attempt.

In guiding users to effectively employ these search engines, this book identifies and explains those areas, such as query design and evaluative techniques, in which you can exercise significant control. We have tested and tried to verify each tool's claims about its own abilities—sometimes with very surprising results. These results are presented—from a user's perspective—in evaluations of seven different search engines' performance. The criteria we used to evaluate each tool can be found on pages 43–44. To exemplify the purposes and behaviors of the primary components that comprise a search engine, this *Guide* also introduces a generic model search engine. The individual search engine evaluations are intended to help you search the tools available *now*; the generic model will help you better understand how today's tools work, as well as how to evaluate and use future versions of these tools and their competitors.

HOW THIS *GUIDE* IS ORGANIZED

Section I briefly discusses how the Web developed and explains its underlying architecture and composition. A general understanding of HTTP, browsers, and other Web basics is essential to understanding effective Web searching.

Section II presents our generic search tool model, which is based on some inescapable functions common to all Web search tools: (1) identifying and collecting new documents from the Web, (2) reformatting and/or indexing new document content to integrate with the existing collection, (3) storing large amounts of data, (4) querying and analyzing the resulting database, and (5) providing a user interface for query input and output. Notice that except for the first, these functions apply to any electronic retrieval mechanism, from electronic address books to online library catalogs. This Section focuses on how Web search tools *in particular* have added to and implemented these functions in today's rapidly changing global network environment. The Web's automated robots, flashy interfaces, ranking algorithms, advertising, and many other innovations mark the arrival of a striking new breed of retrieval tools with all of the problems and promises of their forebears—plus some new ones.

Section III provides detailed descriptions and evaluations of seven specific search engines: AltaVista, Excite, Hotbot, Infoseek, Lycos, Open Text, and WebCrawler. All seven conform to the model we developed in Section II. Although these tools change rapidly (and often unexpectedly), such changes very rarely significantly alter the search experience (in fact, most changes involve redesigning the user interface on a purely cosmetic level). Nonetheless, we concentrate on those facets of the tools that are the least subject to change, yet are the most significant for retrieval. The analyses and evaluations of robot harvesting styles, indexing techniques, database content (relative to competitors), ranking quality, and other features presented in this Section paint an informative picture of the enduring strengths and weaknesses of these seven popular engines.

Section IV contains important observations and suggestions for understanding how Web search tools relate to their environment, including an exploration of how their economic environment affects both users and the future development of the tools themselves. The *Guide*'s final chapter briefly addresses several other tools like Yahoo! that organize and retrieve Web sites and documents, but do not conform to our generic model because they employ human editorial control over some part of the harvesting and indexing processes. This Chapter identifies some information needs for which these sorts of tools can be more effective than search engines.

USING SEARCH TOOLS

The *Neal-Schuman Authoritative Guide to Web Search Engines* is intended to be a descriptive and evaluative assessment of search engines, but is primarily written as a working searcher's guide on how best to evaluate and exploit any search engine. As such, we encourage you to use it to:

- make informed selections of the search engines described and others;
- help formulate your searches;
- help interpret your search results; and
- help evaluate new search engines or new versions of old ones.

We hope you will find the *Guide* to be as interesting and informative as we found compiling it to be.

SECTION I

ESSENTIAL BACKGROUND

Chapter 1

Introduction to the World Wide Web

HOW THE WEB DEVELOPED

The U.S. Department of Defense created the Advanced Research Projects Agency (ARPA) in 1969 to develop and maintain methods of automated communication control capable of operating during domestic emergencies. The agency responded with ARPAnet, a distributed computing communications network. Unlike other networks of its time, ARPAnet could communicate with multiple computer platforms. It was designed to monitor and switch between a host of electronic pathways, to maintain open lines of communication independent of the availability of particular paths and nodes. The effect was that of a web of overlapping lines and connecting nodes, distributed across the country, connecting any two nodes through multiple channels. These multiplatform and multichannel methods of communications eventually became known as the Transmission Control Protocol and Internet Protocol (TCP/IP), which largely define the Internet as it stands today. TCP/IP provides a common format for encoding and transmitting data between different computers.

During the 1980s, the National Science Foundation (NSF) expanded its network (NSFnet) in an attempt to increase international educational and research opportunities. Although modeled on ARPAnet, this network used NSF's computers for e-mail, file transfer, and data storage. NSFnet, incorporating TCP/IP, evolved into the Internet.

As NSFnet expanded into the public sector and became the Internet, there was increasing need for better access tools. Gopher, Veronica, Archie, and WAIS were all attempts to provide more order and searchability for information on the Internet. Each new round of tools made it possible to link more information into the networks. Increasing ease of use and cheaper computing power drew in more information providers, creating many more nodes and expanding the existing ones.

This rapid expansion made it impossible for NSF to control NSFnet as an exclusively nonprofit educational and research resource. During the late 1980s and early 1990s, private and commercial spheres replaced researchers as the primary Internet users. NSF worked with the Department of Commerce to transfer financial backing of the Internet to the private sector.

In 1989 Tim Berners-Lee of CERN, the European Laboratory for Particle Physics near Geneva, developed HTTP (Hypertext Transfer Protocol), the basis for a graphical interface to the Internet. Coupled with HTML (Hypertext Markup Language), a simple mark-up language for viewing and linking documents, HTTP facilitated the creation of the World Wide Web (WWW). The Web began its explosive growth in 1993 with the release of Mosaic, developed and freely distributed by the National Center for Supercomputing Applications (NCSA) at the University of Illinois at Urbana-Champaign. Mosaic was the first Web browser, a software package that runs on the user's PC, communicating with document servers and translating Web page HTML codes and text into a display for the user. Mosaic offered an easy way to view and navigate the Web, using its hypertext and graphical capabilities.

HTTP and Telnet

HTTP (Hypertext Transfer Protocol) is the standard syntax that defines how information is transmitted across the Web. HTTP is stateless—it maintains no permanent connection between the user's PC and the server (the distant computer on which a Web page resides). HTTP opens a TCP/IP connection that lasts only long enough to transport a request and corresponding response. Once the document reaches the user's personal computer (PC) the connection is closed. Other protocols, like Telnet, maintain the connection between the user's PC and the server, transferring continuous streams of information between the two ends. Using Telnet, the user's PC only relays the information from the server to the user as it receives it—the user's machine acts like a "dumb terminal," storing nothing in its own memory. HTTP rations bandwidth on the Internet, by limiting the connection to pairs of requests and answers for files. The HTTP server depends on a "smart client" to store the answer to each request in its own memory, so that it can continue to display the results to the user, without the server's constant retransmission. This allows the Web to transfer large files (such as graphics) and handle large amounts of traffic, without using as many resources as Telnet.

The Internet arose primarily to handle text-based information, using the TCP/IP protocols. The World Wide Web incorporates the same protocols as the rest of the Internet, but HTTP offers a stateless connection that saves bandwidth, allowing authors to link pages containing large multimedia files. When the user clicks on a hypertext link, the personal computer (PC) sends an HTTP request to the server named in the link, which responds by sending an HTTP message containing a single copy of the appropriate Web page. The user's PC stores this copy of the Web page in its own memory for continued display to the user, rather than relaying a continuous broadcast (like a radio signal) from the server on which the page resides. The latter approach describes the Telnet style of network connection, where the server does not use the PC's resources. Instead, Telnet treats the PC as a "dumb terminal" which can only relay communication from the distant machine to the user's screen, with no manipulation of the data. Telnet maintains state, meaning it keeps an open connection between the user's machine and the data server, while HTTP is stateless, relying on brief intermittent connections (independent of one another) for each message the machines send. One way to visualize this is to imagine a smart radio able to request a song from a station and receive it as a single brief message. The smart radio can save the song and play it repeatedly for the listener, independent of what the radio station is transmitting later. This radio does not maintain a continuous receiving-then-playing connection with the station's broadcast.

Although the Internet is composed of many things, at its most basic level, standards and protocols define it. The widespread, uniform employment of these standards allows the heterogeneous population of computers on the Internet to communicate. We have mentioned HTML, HTTP, TCP/IP, and Telnet. Other standards and protocols include URLs (Uniform Resource Locators), standard methods for addressing files on the Internet; FTP (File Transfer Protocol), for transferring files of any type between machines; and Gopher, for organizing documents into a browsable, hierarchical structure. The International Engineering Task Force (IETF) and the World Wide Web Organization (W3O) are two leading organizations of computing professionals voluntarily collaborating to develop standards, software, and technology for the Web. Similar bodies include CERN, MIT, and other institutions in higher education.

The growing commercial interest in the WWW has implications for both its structure and content. The Web standards-setting bodies, such as IETF and W3O, play their roles almost by default. No single organization controls the creation of rules and upgrading schedules. Consequently, the process of setting up new standards is usually slow and complicated. As the number of Web users and content providers explodes, however, standards-setting bodies are finding it more difficult to respond to their demands. Commercial interests are already beginning to respond.

A perfect example of such a commercial interest is Netscape. Netscape created its Web browser software to take advantage of standards (HTML, HTTP) that preceded it. As Netscape developed new features for its product (such as frames in Web pages), however, the HTML standard was not revised to incorporate the change. Netscape continued to tinker with the HTML standard and distribute its revisions. Given the ubiquity of Netscape's browser, many authors decided the new features were worth adding to their own pages. Once usage had spread widely enough, Netscape's browser became a de facto, "common law" HTML standard. Further innovations and continued investment in the Web undoubtedly will produce similar scenarios in the future.

WEB CONTENT

Although the information on the Web may encompass as many subjects as a library, two categories of information naturally present themselves: that which is freely, publicly available, and that which is accessible only for a fee. Fee-based and proprietary information makes up only a small percentage of the Web material indexed by public search tools. We will not cover fee-based sources in much detail, except to offer an example. Information provided by many traditional commercial database vendors, such as Dialog, is now accessible through the Web. Users must still establish accounts and pay for the opportunity to search Dialog's databases, but they can log in and search through a Dialog Web page. Vendors may use different interfaces and search-and-retrieval software on the Web from that of their traditional environments, but they usually offer the same databases. Thus pay services still represent a valuable resource accessible *through* the Web but the content is not available using Web indexes like those we will discuss.

Whereas fee-based Web content usually involves the more traditional bibliographic databases and news files, free information on the Web covers everything else imaginable. It is cheap and easy for someone who already has access to a PC and a phone line to publish information on the Web. Both individuals and major groups (including governments, educational institutions, large and small businesses, nonprofit and professional organizations) have already contributed content to the Web. The range of subjects and quality of the information covers everything conceivably associated with these groups—and more. The Web does not provide any centralized or consistent organizational scheme for this information, however, unlike more familiar sources.

The Web and the indexes of its content do not replace or duplicate traditional information resources. Even with a perfect search-and-retrieval tool (and there is not one), the Web does not offer the depth or authority of sources like *Science Citation Index* or MEDLINE. Standard reference tools require a great deal of organization and significant resources to produce and maintain. They also focus on information related by predefined subjects and disciplines, rather than on a random body of documents. The fruits of these labors are not free, even when the Web offers a cheaper medium than print. The Web can, however, offer things like citations (or even the entire text of articles and manuscripts) too new to have made it into major indexes. Fringe literature (produced outside the major research and publishing communities) has a large presence on the Web. A good example is new age medicine, especially alternative (and often questionable) treatments for cancer and AIDS. Since the Web offers the freedom to publish outside the usual channels, it can avoid both unfair biases and sound criticism involved with the traditional publishing industry. The Web is thus an exciting and interesting complement to traditional information sources.

Some of the most valuable information on the Web is produced by the government, from census data to pending legislation. Since there are usually no copyright restrictions or print sales to contend with, government research, reprints, transcripts, and archives are readily available, although even in these cases authenticity is sometimes an issue. It is easy to acquire a government document online (usually in simple ASCII text format), revise it, and place it on another site. Although this is probably illegal, and definitely unscrupulous, it is a simple prank to accomplish. Users should always scan for false or mischievous content on the Web and searchers should verify sources whenever possible.

Educational resources available on the Web range from university admissions forms and class schedules to local elementary cafeteria menus and bus routes to progress reports on new research. Businesses and professional organizations often have a home page with brief histories, product information, financial data, and press releases. General business resources include stock prices, major newspapers and magazines, and employment bulletin boards.

Recreational and entertainment sites abound. In fact this is arguably the Web's most successful arena. Reference tools and forums devote themselves to every imaginable hobby, fan club, collectible, author—you name it. State parks, theme parks, local tourism boards, national monuments, and sports teams all have Web sites to please fans and attract new ones, and major events like the Olympics are sure to have Web pages, even if they are only temporary.

So what is *not* on the Web? Until recently no copyrighted document or item published and sold in print format was freely accessible (at least not *legally*) on the Web. This is still a good rule of thumb for the searcher, but more printed and copyrighted publications are popping up free to the user. Some publishers consider Web editions good enough advertising to offset potential lost print sales—for example, many daily comic strips are available on the Web, as are some magazines and newspapers. Also, some publishers sell their content to a vendor who then places it on a Web site supported by third-party advertisers—users have free access, as long as advertisers succeed in reaching an audience.

HOW DO YOU FIND INFORMATION ON THE WEB?

So how does a new Web user learn what is out there? There are three ways to find information on the Web. First, there is serendipitous discovery. Web documents contain links to other Web documents. Once users have a page to start from, they can begin following links in any direction. A friend's Web page may link to a movie review catalog, which links to a particular movie studio home page, which links to an actor's biographical page, which links to a tourism page in the actor's country of origin. Users can follow such a set of links in less than a minute and discover quite a lot; however, if the original desire was to find the tourist page, and the user did not know how to get there from the starting point, this strategy is inadequate.

Subject guides, such as Yahoo! and Magellan, provide a second, much more useful method of finding pages dealing with specific subjects. Most of these tools employ human indexers to evaluate Web pages and place them in an appropriate position on a hierarchical subject tree. Similar to library shelf classification schemes, the subject trees guide users through sets of links representing different levels of subject specificity. Pets could lead to Cats, leading to Feeding, leading finally to a list of Dietary Guidelines for Domestic Cats. These subject guides are great places to find quality pages on many subjects, but they cannot evaluate or include the vast majority of pages on the Web, simply because of the size of the task. Also, this method of organizing documents sacrifices much of the flexibility of the Web's hypertext environment by imposing a traditional hierarchical structure. Users are at the mercy of the indexers' sense of what information belongs where.

A third option for retrieving Web pages is using a search engine—our focus for the rest of this book. Search engines such as Excite, HotBot, Infoseek, WebCrawler, Open Text, Lycos, and AltaVista use automatic indexing software to discover, harvest, and index Web pages. They provide a Web page interface for users to type keyword or natural language queries, and they provide search results as pages of links, which the user may follow to actual documents on the Web. Although these tools are all far from perfect, they provide access to significant chunks of the Web. Used well and in conjunction with one another, these tools are valuable resources.

Searching the Web with online search engines can be confusing, however. Different search engines produce different results for the same query, and they provide a variety of search options and interfaces, yet still claim to be providing the "best" search of "the Web." Much of this confusion clears once one realizes that user queries are searches of databases created and maintained by robots that harvest only some of the information on the Web, using a variety of approaches. In Section II we discuss each of the primary components common to all of the Web search tools that we evaluate in Section III. These primary components are robots (software that identify and index Web pages), indexes (databases of words taken from Web pages, and the addresses of the pages that contain them), interfaces (the part of the tool with which the user directly interacts), and search engines (software programs that search the index for words in the user's query).

SECTION II

A MODEL SEARCH TOOL

Chapter 2

Robots

HISTORY OF AUTOMATED WEB SEARCHING

Before we get into specific search engines, we think it is important to discuss the evolution of the species. When the Web first became available to the public, the only way to navigate it was by "surfing" with a text-only browser (Lynx). Users began with a known page and launched forth from the links it contained, browsing until they found something. When there were only a couple hundred HTTP servers on the Internet, this method could work. Most of these machines contained centrally managed collections of documents for students and professional researchers who were aware of the major repositories of information in their fields. The rapid growth of the Web both in the numbers and kinds of resources available (and the numbers and kinds of users of those resources) created a need for better ways of organizing information on the Web.

The first attempts to impose order on the Web involved manually creating master lists of page links in hierarchical subject categories. The World Wide Web Consortium (W3C) maintained one such list. Yahoo! began as a simple list of popular links (although it has since expanded its content and services considerably). The growth of the Web has proven much too fast, however, for small pockets of human indexers to keep up with it in any comprehensive fashion. The Web's sheer size prevents much human control of the collection and indexing of Web pages. People can and do create small databases of Web resources, but gathering *all* of the information available is impossible. Large-scale indexing requires automated means.

Martijn Koster led an early project to index the contents of Web servers. He combined human and automated effort to produce ALIWEB (Archie-Like Indexing of the WEB).[1] First available to the public in October 1993, ALIWEB put the indexing responsibility squarely on the shoulders of local server operators, or webmasters. To have resources indexed in ALIWEB, a webmaster had to create and maintain a special ALIWEB file, describing the site's contents, on his or her server. ALIWEB would then use fully automated robot software to travel the Web searching for these special files. As it discovered them, the robot would compile their contents (lists of Web pages) into an index. Not surprisingly, few webmasters bothered to create and maintain ALIWEB files for their servers.

Most of the robots used in the search engines that we review are proprietary products. The companies that develop and sell them are generally reluctant to provide specific information about how their robots work. Koster, however, placed the code for ALIWEB's automated robots on the Internet. Soon other programmers modified these robots to perform more complicated and ambitious tasks. Also referred to as *spiders, worms, crawlers,* and *intelligent agents,* these new robots are programs designed to retrieve actual Web pages for indexing. Whereas ALIWEB only retrieved specially designed files listing groups of pages, the next generation of robots could discover the pages for themselves, and even harvest information from the HTML <BODY> of the text of those pages. A robot can be subject-specific, seeking any page containing certain key words or phrases, or it can be site-specific, looking exclusively for pages in particular locations. In fact, simple parameter variations allow robots to be customized to search for almost anything on the Web. It is even possible for users to employ their own personal Web spider, which hunts down information about favorite topics and brings home the spoils. For our discussion, however, we will be concerned only with robots that attempt to gather everything they can find on the Web, to create large general-purpose public indexes.

The World Wide Web Worm (also known as WWWW, W4, or the Worm) was one of the first publicly accessible search tools to appear on the Web. The Worm used its robots to discover documents and index their URLs (Uniform Resource Locators) and <TITLE>s (i.e., the text in the Web pages marked with HTML <TITLE> tags). First available in February 1994, the Worm was developed at the University of Colorado's computer science department by Oliver McBryan.

The Worm was based on a theory similar to citation searching. It treated URLs (in the form of hypertext links) as citations to Web pages. The Worm's database contained only Web pages that were linked from other Web pages, in an effort to capitalize on an author's judgment that another page was worth referencing. It indexed the URLs, disassembling them into component words that were stored together so that users could retrieve the associated pages using keyword searches. It was hoped that, by limiting the index exclusively to URLs and <TITLE>s, the Worm would be able to keep up with the rapid growth of the Web without using a prohibitively large amount of resources.

The Worm was a big improvement over its predecessors in Web retrieval technology. It offered a way to create a database of Web pages with no external human intervention. No person had to tell the robot which documents to index, and the user did not have to rely as much on serendipitous links to find relevant information. A user search would produce results in the form of a unique set of <TITLE>s and URLs hotlinked to the original documents on their home servers. The downside was that the Worm did rely on Web page authors to employ descriptive <TITLE>s and URLs. If a specific document's <TITLE> or URL did not contain sufficiently descriptive information, it was next to impossible to search with the Worm and retrieve it.

The Worm was quickly followed by search tools boasting robots that could index the text *within* Web documents, rather than just the <TITLE>s and URLs assigned to those documents. The RBSE (Repository Based Software Engineering) Spider was one of the first.[2] RBSE consisted of two robots—one for finding and gathering URLs and a second for retrieving and indexing the documents associated with each URL. This approach offered users the chance to retrieve documents by searching their actual content.

By the summer of 1994, search tools were popping up all over the Web. The next major tools were WebCrawler and Lycos, which established the pattern for most of the search engines reviewed in Section III. The remainder of Section II describes how a Web search tool is created and searched. We create a simple model of a generic search tool (composed of an imaginary robot, index, and databases) to illustrate four basic functions common to all of the current breed:

- finding Web pages (this chapter)
- harvesting Web pages and building an index (Chapter 3)
- searching the index with a user query (Chapter 3)
- providing the user interface (Chapter 4)

Robots are essential ingredients of all current Web search tools. Robots perform a wide variety of tasks, only some of which are related to the Web. Their more common uses include

- discovering Web pages for inclusion in a database
- indexing Web pages
- measuring the size and scope of the Web
- maintaining a database of Web pages by checking old links for updates and relocation
- mirroring sites (i.e., duplicating the structure and content of popular sites on other servers)

Some robots perform two or more of these duties. The following section describes how robots perform the first of these functions.

HOW ROBOTS DISCOVER RESOURCES ON THE WEB

The *WWW Robot FAQ*[3] defines a Web robot as "a program that automatically traverses the Web's hypertext structure by retrieving a document and recursively retrieving all documents that are referenced." This process is similar to a citation search, in that links between Web documents are treated as citations to be followed. For example, a student who encounters a reference within a textbook to a journal article offering a deeper discussion of a concept may stop and track down the article before returning to the rest of the textbook. Many robots behave analogously: they begin with the first hypertext link in a known document, follow that link wherever it leads for a while, and then return to the original document to launch forth again from the next link.

It is important to remember that a robot is a software program located on a specific machine. We may describe its activities as "traveling," "hunting," "exploring," and so forth, but a robot does not actually *go* anywhere. More accurately, it uses HTTP to request documents associated with particular URLs from servers on the Web—the same sort of function a browser performs when a user clicks on a link in a Web page. HTTP uses a stateless connection, which means that when two machines communicate with it, there is no persistent connection between them. This communication is composed of a discrete request (from the client machine) and a response (from the server). One way of visualizing this interaction is as rapid e-mail communication, initiated by a message from the client and concluded by a reply from the server. HTTP opens a TCP/IP connection between the two machines, then closes it after a request and response have passed through.

OUR DISCOVERY ROBOT

In order to create our own index of Web pages, we must first create a robot that can find documents. The Web is huge and growing rapidly. Documents are added and removed, updated and revised, renamed and relocated every minute of every day. Our Web robot has to be fast enough to keep up with this growth. Most search tools speed the process of discovery by employing multiple robots of different types. The more robots crawling the Web, the better their chances of keeping up. To keep our example simple, however, we will only use one (hypothetical) robot for document discovery and try to maximize its performance. We call our robot Steve (which is in no way derived from the word *spider*).

In addition to documents in HTML, ASCII, and other text formats, the Web contains numeric databases, software programs, and multimedia files incorporating sound, pictures, and movies. Steve will be configured to retrieve all such files in all formats. Even though such files may not contain any text to index, Steve can still note the format of the file and the URL (which may contain descriptive text). In addition to HTTP space, the Web links other parts of the Internet, such as Gopher space, Usenet, FTP (File Transfer Protocol) sites, and

Telnet sites. Steve will travel through Gopher and FTP, but will bypass Telnet sites (they are tough for robots to connect to) and Usenet (Usenet grows much more rapidly than the Web—it is composed of messages and pieces of electronic conversations resembling e-mail more than Web pages—and is too tough for Steve to keep track of). It is important to remember, however, that Steve will collect Gopher and FTP documents *only if they are referenced from a Web document*; Steve will not make a concerted effort to index all of Gopher and FTP space. This rule is also true for most of the Web search tools we review later. Thus a user conducting a full search for FTP and Gopher documents would be forced to use the search tools designed for those environments—Archie and Veronica.

Archie and Veronica

Archie and Veronica search FTP sites and Gopher space, respectively. FTP (File Transfer Protocol) is a method of transferring text and binary files from point to point over the Internet. FTP sites contain everything from text files to computer programs to pictures, but visitors have no way of examining the contents of those files until they download them to their own computers. FTP offers only the short file name and the hierarchical file structure of the server to identify documents. Archie indexes the names of those files and offers keyword searches of the index to users. Gopher software enables system administrators to store text files in a hierarchical structure on a server. These files can be local resources (stored on that computer) or links to other servers. Users view the files and links via a Telnet connection. Veronica (Very Easy Rodent Oriented Net-wide Index to Computerized Archives) offers user searches of Gopher file titles.

We also have several options for how Steve will discover these documents. All discovery robots must begin searching from some active page on the Web, preferably one with a variety of links to follow. Beginning with the first link on such a page, Steve can undertake either a depth-first or a breadth-first strategy.

A depth-first strategy would send Steve to the page attached to the first link on the initial page, then to the page on the first link of the second page, then to the first link on the third page, and so forth. Steve evaluates each link that he tries and chooses either to store the URL for a later visit (to index it) or to discard it. He evaluates links based on any of a variety of possible criteria, such as whether the page contains indexable text or whether or not the robot has already encountered the page in previous wanderings. When he finally reaches a dead end, either by attempting to follow a link to a page that is no longer available or by accessing a page that contains no outward links, Steve takes one step back to the page he last visited and follows the next available link.

In the breadth-first strategy, Steve takes one step backward after each step forward. He follows the first link on the initial page, then retreats to follow the second link on that same page. He continues in this manner until he has gathered or discarded all of the URLs of the links on the first page—only then does he move on to the page associated with the first link, where he will begin methodically grabbing the URLs of links on the new page.

The prevailing belief is that depth-first gathering creates a relatively comprehensive database on a few subjects, while breadth-first indexing builds databases touching more lightly on a wider variety of documents. This belief arises from the common hierarchical arrangement of documents in computers and other information systems (such as classification schemes and call numbers in libraries).

Computer directories and subdirectories usually reflect the tendency of the human mind to group like items together. A directory usually contains files related to one another, as well as subdirectories to hold files that have been further grouped into subclasses. The Dewey Decimal Classification (DDC) system defines ten classes of knowledge by which to organize books on library shelves. DDC incorporates four volumes of rules for creating smaller groups within these ten major categories to indefinite levels of specificity. In both libraries and computers (to varying degrees), users may begin at the top level of any class or directory and move steadily downward through levels of ever greater specificity, which provide increasingly detailed and magnified views of a single subject. Thus one may travel from *Mammals* to *Dogs* to *Beagles* on the shelves, before jumping back up to *Fish* and on down to *Sharks* and then *Great White Sharks*. Most of the files used by word-processing programs will reside in a single directory on a hard drive, further grouped within subdirectories and sub-subdirectories by similarities in their formats and functions. This creates a somewhat ad hoc classification structure.

On the Internet, server administrators arrange and maintain FTP resources as individual repositories with strict organizational structures. FTP sites have a vested interest in maintaining a clear hierarchical directory structure, since visitors cannot look directly into a file to identify its content without downloading it. To ensure that the structure remains intact, administrators severely limit access to the structure of FTP directories. Gopher sites also tend to have strict centralized control and a standard hierarchical organizational structure; however, Gopher space, like the Web, incorporates hypertext, linking documents between disparate sites and introducing a chaotic character that coexists with the more traditional structure.

While many Web servers are wholly maintained by a single person or a small group of administrators, many more are not. One of the more highly touted aspects of the Web is its accessibility. Anyone can pay a minimal fee to an access provider and post a Web page, or a cluster of interlocking pages that are further linked to almost any other point on the Web. Authors can put almost anything in their pages, in any order, and name these pages any way they like. The cumulative result is the Web, a huge repository of data, organized (or disorganized, depending on your perspective) every which way at once. Starting from any initial point on the Web, one can launch forth to almost any other point.

If the vision of this twisting maze of information is daunting to the human Web user, imagine the predicament facing a simple robot, which has essentially no powers of semantic understanding. Remember that the theories of depth- and breadth-first gathering assume that the information proximal to a Web page (for example, the pages that inhabit the same server, or that are connected over distance through shared links) is related to it. The Web embodies, at best, a cracked mirror image of such hierarchical structure. Even when links do branch out into logical hierarchies and make perfect sense to a conscious observer, the shift in "direction" (required of the observer's point of view) among overlapping structures is simply beyond the abilities of current robots.

While human users may be able to interpret rapidly shifting contexts and perspectives as they jump around the Web, Steve must rely on the careful forethought of webmasters and authors to clump information into a consistent structure that matches his searching strategy. Many Web pages and servers are well organized. Yet Steve's path is clearly a rocky one; one of the Web's creators originally proposed the environment as "Human-readable information linked together in an unconstrained way."[4] The original purpose of the Web was to escape some of the historical structures imposed on information; a search tool's purpose is to attempt to restore some order.

Neither of these two gathering strategies actually performs predictably over the Web as a whole, although either strategy may be employed to different ends for greater effect. For example, if we wish to create a subject-specific index, our best bet would be to select a known relevant group of pages to explore, rather than one initial document, and employ a depth-first strategy with an upper bound on the degree of depth. Thus Steve would travel a predefined maximum distance from his starting point before returning to try another path. This would prevent him from becoming lost in inevitable digressions, while exploring a largely unknown space in some depth. On the other hand, if we wish to build an index that samples the wide variety of the Web, we might well choose a breadth-first strategy, with biases toward short URLs and URLs from previously unexplored servers. Using this approach, Steve would be more likely to sample a lot of disparate points on the Web, so that users could find a relevant starting point for surfing deeper on any given topic.

Most of the Web search tools that we review use some variation of the breadth-first gathering strategy, to provide somewhat relevant materials on a wide variety of topics to satisfy the heterogeneous population of Web users. Such a strategy will quickly sample most servers connected to the Web before exploring their nooks and crannies. Steve will behave this way, too.

For his first hunt, Steve could either start with a small database of URLs that we have handpicked from multiple known servers on the Web, or he could begin with a single page linked to a variety of other pages on many different Web servers. Many robots start from Netscape's What's New or What's Cool pages. Since "new" and "cool" are hardly restrictive subject categories, these pages serve as good jumping-off points to unrelated information, often pages that are popular links for other Web authors.

Steve starts with the What's New page. The first link he encounters on the Netscape page is to the Australian Internet Awards. Steve notes the URL associated with the link (*www.webawards.info.au*) and stores it in the database. The

AT&T 1996 Olympic Games Connection follows the Australians, and Steve dutifully stores the URL for this second link. This process continues until Steve reaches the last link on *What's New*—the Weight Watchers home page (*www.weightwatchers.com*). Having mined the Netscape page, he steps back, looks at his new collection of URLs, chooses one, then visits that page to gather its links as well. In theory, the process continues until Steve has followed every possible link.

USING THE URL DATABASE

Once he builds a database of URLs to work with, Steve must decide how to choose among them for his next excursion. He could simply choose the first URL he found (*www.webawards.info.au*), he could blindly choose one at random, or he could rank them by any of a variety of preferences. Each Web search tool has its robots approach this step differently. Steve ranks the URLs according to his own unique combination of preferences, yet the factors he considers are common ones.

First Steve compares the URLs in the database to identify (and eliminate) duplicates. This process is probably not necessary for his first batch of URLs gathered from the same page, but Steve must think long-term—he will soon have a huge database of URLs from links all over the Web, and duplicates could be a big problem. His first step will be to alphabetize the URLs, so that duplicates will lie next to one another for easy elimination.

Next, in a similar move, Steve compares the URLs to identify new *servers*. Even though our database may contain 100 URLs of 100 unique pages, those pages could reside on as many as 100 different servers or on just one. Our desire for a wide variety of information forces Steve to prefer pages on machines that he has never visited; those pages will rise further up the queue than pages from familiar servers. Once again, this issue becomes more important as Steve gradually encounters fewer strange machines. At the moment, Steve has visited very few servers, so they all offer him a variety of new pages; but as Steve roams the Internet, he will get to know most of the available servers and what they have to offer. Since he will still prefer novel content, it becomes increasingly essential that he give top priority to new sites as he discovers them.

Steve identifies the server on which a Web page lives by looking at the domain name, the first part of the URL. The domain name is the part of the URL just to the right of the "http://" that uses periods for punctuation rather than semicolons or slashes. Since the URLs are already in alphabetical order, pages on the same server (that is, with the same domain name) will be grouped together. For example,

> *www.webawards.info.au/home.html*
> *www.weightwatchers.com/exercise/aerobics/classes.html*
> *www.weightwatchers.com/exercise/swimming/classes.html*
> *www.weightwatchers.com/food/cooking/classes.html*

are URLs for four different pages, listed in alphabetical order. The last three URLs are all from the same server, whose domain name is *www.weightwatchers.com*. The first URL is from a different server, named *www.webawards.info.au*. Steve identifies these two unique servers from the four URLs. If he has visited one of them in the past, but not the other, he will visit the new one first.

Steve extends this same line of reasoning to evaluate the length of URLs. Just as we assume that different servers are likely to hold different content, we assume that the files in distinct branches of the file structure of a single Web server will also differ. We can turn this theory into practice with Steve, since the URL, in its capacity as a "locator" or address, provides a glimpse of a page's position in its server's structure. For example,

www.weightwatchers.com

is in all likelihood the top page, or home page, of the Weight Watcher's site. It contains links to pages deeper in the file structure dealing with the variety of concepts Weight Watchers involves. On the other hand,

www.weightwatchers.com/exercise/aerobics/classes.html

describes a page listing aerobics classes. Other pages cover swimming classes (*www.weightwatchers.com/exercise/swimming/classes.html*) or, in the food neighborhood, cooking classes (*www.weightwatchers.com/food/cooking/classes.html*).

Notice that the longer the URL grows, the deeper in the classification scheme the page lies, and the more specific the subject matter becomes. Notice, too, that these pages, although multiple levels apart in the file structure of the server, are also all of a single type: they are lists of available classes. On the shelves of a library, these documents would either stand next to one another as a group of course offerings, or apart with groups of other documents on their respective subjects (cooking, swimming, and aerobics). On the Web, however, from the perspective of the user or a robot, these pages could do both. In addition to links connecting the pages hierarchically to their respective subjects, another page (*www.weightwatchers.com/classes.html*) can directly link them together as a major category on par with food and exercise.

It is this enviably flexible structure of interlocking relationships that makes the hypertext environment so liberating. Yet this same characteristic undermines our forethought in designing a methodical robot, by shifting perspectives and throwing duplicate routes to the same documents in the robot's path. Nevertheless, Steve must decide what URL to start with somehow, and the shorter URL is still the safest bet for achieving our breadth-first goals.

Recall that Steve discovered every URL from the initial Netscape page that he visited. There are a couple of reasons why we do not want him to be quite so thorough every time. First, our desire to visit as much of the Web and to gather as wide a variety of documents as possible is not satisfied by dwelling on a single page or server for very long. Since Steve will eventually revisit most sites for repeated harvesting and updates, we can widen his search pattern by having him gather only a percentage of the links from a single source during each visit. For instance, he could retrieve every third link, rather than every link. In fact, most robots only pull a sample percentage of the links from a single source.

Besides its strategic value, there is another reason for using this sampling approach—diplomacy. Steve must keep in mind the effect he has on other servers. An automatic robot can request documents from a server hundreds of times per second. A rapid-fire series of requests to the same server can crash it (shut the server down temporarily). To avoid this, Steve will only gather a percentage of the documents at a site. He will also wait a full minute between requests. This gives servers some breathing room, and also helps decrease overall congestion on the Web.

"Netiquette" for Robots

One aspect to being a good Web neighbor is respecting servers' privacy. Some servers may contain sensitive or copyrighted information, or they may not be able to handle much traffic. Whatever the reason, some servers want robots to leave them alone. If this is the case, the administrator can insert a file named robots.txt into the root directory of the server. The file contains restrictions on a visiting robot's behavior, or a warning to stay away completely. Robots are expected to obey this Robot Exclusion Protocol; although this protocol has no force of law, it is widely recognized "netiquette."

Now that our URL database is a little cleaner and Steve has identified the best servers to start with, we turn to a second robot to build our searchable index. The index (composed of words from Web pages) is what the search engine compares with keywords from the user's query. The keywords are linked to a second database containing the summaries and <TITLE>s of Web pages, which make up a user's search results. Together with the user interface, these pieces constitute the part of the search tool with which the user interacts.

NOTES

1. ALIWEB's main site is currently http://web.nexor.co.uk/public/aliweb/aliweb.html.
2. http://rbse.jsc.nasa.gov/Spider/search.html
3. http://info.webcrawler.com/mak/projects/robots/faq.html#what
4. http://www.w3.org/pub/WWW/History/1989/proposal.html

Chapter 3

Building and Searching the Index

This chapter is a general description of how Web search tools create and search their indexes and databases. It is *general* to provide an inclusive context for using any of the variety of current and future Web search tools. A broad understanding of the structure and features of these resources will enable readers to evaluate and exploit both current and future manifestations of Web search tools.

HARVESTING

Recall from the previous chapter that robot software, like Steve, follows hypertext links in the Web, discovers new documents, and saves the addresses of the documents it likes in a URL database. This discovery robot blazes the trail and leaves behind the initial database for a second robot, the harvester.

When the harvester robot comes along, it checks the database of URLs and begins automatically revisiting each Web page the first robot discovered. Instead of just recording the URL, the second robot extracts (harvests) part or all of the text from the page, breaks it down into component words, and integrates it into a master index of words from other Web documents. This is the index that the user searches. Most search tools also create a separate database containing records similar to catalog cards. Each record is composed of a Web page URL, title, and summary. When a user search retrieves a URL, the search tool presents this summary record to the user. Although robots are constantly harvesting documents in this manner, they usually only update the master index on a daily or weekly basis. The information flows like this:

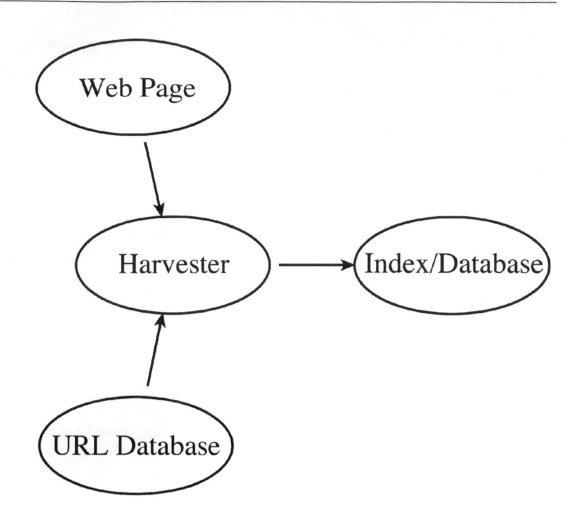

   When users submit a query to a search tool, the tool compares the query to the index that the harvesting agents supply with Web page contents. *Search results are based on the index contents, not on the entire Web.*

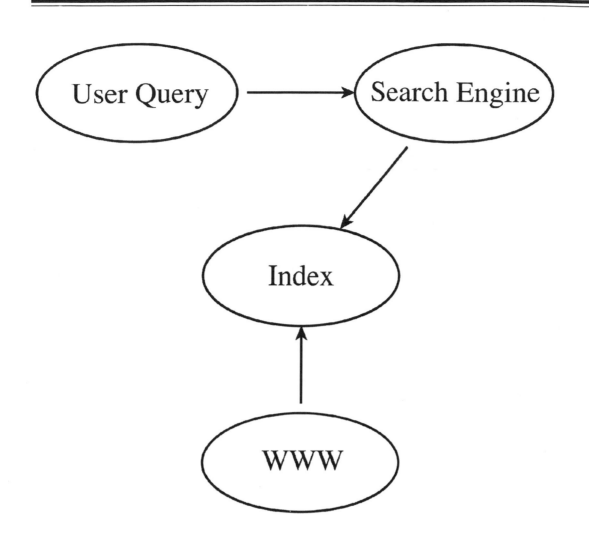

The harvester operates over the whole Web, although it never reaches everything. It takes part of the information that it finds and adds this selected information to the index and the database. The harvester will ignore some pages due to lack of content (such as pages composed of lists of dead links). It will not be able to access other pages either because of technical problems (for example, the server on which the page is stored has gone down) or access restrictions (such as pages that ask robots to leave them alone). Thus a large portion of the Web has not been and will never be indexed.

BUILDING THE INDEX AND DATABASE

Words are the basic units of our sample index. Each word entry in our index has four fields:

- the URL of a page containing the word
- the word's position in the page (i.e., as the first word, second word, etc.)

- the total number of words in the page (in our example this means the sum of the number of words in the <TITLE> and the words in the URL)
- the field in which the word occurs (i.e., <TITLE> or URL)

Our harvester robot updates the index daily. For each new Web page that the robot retrieves, it examines the URL and <TITLE> tag. Most Web search tools also index at least part of the text body from a Web page. To keep our example simple, our harvester only indexes HTML <TITLE>s and URLs. Robots index full text in generally the same manner. The harvester uses a simple list of article, preposition, and special *stopwords* (for example, *a*, *and*, *the*, and *of*). Since these words are typically judged to be of no searching value, they are ignored during indexing and/or searching.

As the harvester reads each word (excluding stopwords) on the Web page, it creates an entry in the database. Using the URLs and <TITLE>s of our examples from the last chapter,

URL	Title
www.webawards.info.au	Australian Internet Awards
www.weightwatchers.com	Weight Watchers Home Page

our harvester creates

Word	Address	Word#	Word Count	Field
Australian	www.webawards.info.au	5	7	Title
Awards	www.webawards.info.au	7	7	Title
com	www.weightwatchers.com	3	7	URL
Home	www.weightwatchers.com	6	7	Title
info	www.webawards.info.au	3	7	URL
Internet	www.webawards.info.au	6	7	Title
Page	www.weightwatchers.com	7	7	Title
Watchers	www.weightwatchers.com	5	7	Title
webawards	www.webawards.info.au	2	7	URL
Weight	www.weightwatchers.com	4	7	Title
weightwatchers	www.weightwatchers.com	2	7	URL
www	www.webawards.info.au	1	7	URL
	www.weightwatchers.com	1	7	URL

The text from each page is parsed, or broken into its component parts—words. The indexing process transforms the information gleaned from the page into a set of words and their positions in the page. The robot defines a word as a string of text surrounded either by a punctuation mark or a blank space. Words begin to the right of a space or punctuation mark and end to the left of a space or punctuation mark. Thus, using the example from Chapter 2, our index includes the word *Internet*, a string of text bounded on either end by two spaces:

Australian **Internet** Awards

It also contains the word *info* since it is bounded by punctuation marks (periods):

www.webawards.**info**.au

The robot calculates each word's position in a page by counting left to right from the first word in the URL to the last word in the <TITLE> field. Thus the word *www* is the first word in both pages in our index:

www.webawards.info.au   Australian Internet Awards
www.weightwatchers.com   Weight Watchers Home Page

In the Australian page, *webawards* is the second word, separated from the first word by a period:

www.**webawards**.info.au   Australian Internet Awards

Indexes that include the full or partial text from the pages they harvest can simply extend this model by continuing to count words through the body of the page (rather than stopping after the <TITLE>), and adding another category (body) to the fields counted.

Web search tools also use other criteria to determine what constitutes a word. Some robots do not index words less than three characters long, automatically omitting some common stopwords, like *to* and *in*. Our indexing process ignores one- and two-letter words. Thus *au* is not in the index; however, when the harvester counted the words in the page, it included *au* in the tally and relative positions. This feature allows users to search the index for phrases and words in certain proximities to one another, even when the phrase includes stopwords.

The word *www* gets a second entry in the index, since it is the one word common to both pages. If *www* also appeared twice in the same page, say at the end of the Weight Watchers <TITLE> (increasing the page's word count from 7 to 8), the entry might look like this:

Word	Address	Word #	Word Count	Field
www	www.webaward.info.au	1	8	URL
	www.weight-watchers.com	8	8	Title
	www.weightwatchers.com	1	7	URL

A more realistically complex index than ours would also keep track of additional statistics for each word, such as the number of pages in which it appears and how many times it appears on each page. These statistics, along with the position number, word count, and field designation are all used extensively for weighting and ranking search results. The field information allows users to restrict searches for keywords to certain parts of a page.

Search tools often take further steps to massage the contents of their indexes. Some automatically truncate words with certain endings or beginning with common roots. For example the word *cats*, taken from a Web page, may be trimmed to *cat* in the index. Since the index does not have to keep track of both words, this saves memory and retrieval time, and also increases the number of results for the user query *cat*. The downside is the lack of precision with which the user can search.

Harvesters generate page summaries automatically. Most simply copy the <TITLE> and a fixed amount of the initial text, perhaps the first 50 words. Other engines, such as those using semantic indexing techniques, weight the words in the text of a Web page, in order to compute the one or two most statistically important sentences in that page. These sentences are then paired with the <TITLE> and stored as the summary record for later presentation to users.

SEARCHING THE INDEX

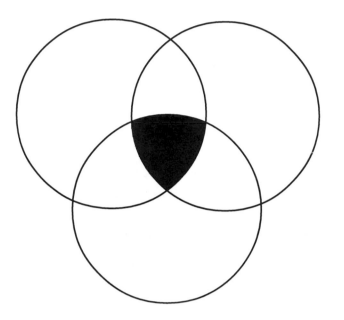

Most queries consist of one or more subject keywords or a natural language statement, either with or without some type of Boolean operator (such as ***AND***) to connect the parts. Once the user types and submits the query, the search engine takes over. The search engine's job is to match the query to the appropriate words in the index. Once the engine finds matching words in the index, it compiles a list of URLs, orders them in some way, and returns the URLs and corresponding summaries to the user. The order in which the URLs are presented in the list is often determined by some type of relevancy ranking, an attempt to move the "hits" most likely to be relevant toward the top.

The search engine begins by breaking the user query into its component pieces, using a variety of algorithms, much as the harvester parses new Web pages. Algorithms are the sets of rules and procedures that determine the search engine's behavior. Each search engine uses a unique set of algorithms to make decisions. Since a superior algorithm is an advantage for a commercial firm, the specific approaches are rarely available to the public. We present some simple algorithms to illustrate how a robot decides to conduct a search.

Our first example search query is

Australian

Since our search statement is a single keyword, the search engine does not have to do much to interpret it. There are no stopwords, operators, or punctuation marks with which to contend, so the engine simply checks the index. It quickly spots **Australian** in the index and notes the one URL associated with it, http://www.webawards.info.au. Next the search engine pulls the record containing the <TITLE> and summary for the Australian Internet Awards page. Since there are no other hits against which to rank the Awards page, the search engine presents the URL, <TITLE>, and summary to the user.

This is a pretty straightforward process. To see where the complications arise, consider the query

Australia* and (www or au)

in which the asterisk acts as a truncation symbol. Now we are hoping to find all pages containing any word beginning with **Australia** in addition to including either **www** or **au**.

First our search algorithm looks for any stopwords to remove from the query. Since our index omits two-letter words, the search engine ignores **au**. Next the engine checks for any special operators attached to the query words. The truncation sign at the end of **Australia*** qualifies. This instructs the search engine to retrieve any words in the index that begin with **Australia**.

The engine next notices the parentheses that determine the order in which it will perform any Boolean operations. Since the search engine will ignore the word **au**, the parenthetical argument simplifies to one word, **www**. The search engine has transformed the query statement into

Australia* and www

The search engine will now look for any page containing both a derivative of **Australia** and the word **www**.

The search engine checks the index for each word of the query individually. As it receives the results for each word, it creates temporary tables to help assemble and order the final list of results. Our search would produce two tables, one for each word:

Word	Address	Word #	Word Count	Field
Australian	www.webaward.info.au	5	7	Title

Word	Address	Word #	Word Count	Field
www	www.webaward.info.au	1	7	URL
	www.weightwatchers.com	1	7	URL

If our index contained more pages, each of these temporary tables would probably contain more than one URL to consider. As it is, our search engine has a relatively easy job comparing the two tables.

Since the simplified user query specifies that resulting pages contain both words, the engine checks the two tables for any matches. It finds one, www. webawards.info.au, and creates a second type of temporary table:

Address	Number of Keywords Found	Number of Times Each Keyword Appears	Fields Where Keywords Occur
www.webawards.info.au	2	1,1	Title,URL

The basic unit of this new table is not the words in the query, but the URLs of the pages that the query has retrieved. Each retrieved page gets an entry in the table, containing such statistics as how many of the keywords it matched from the search, how many occurrences of those words it contains, and in which fields the words appear. These characteristics are the raw data for the ranking algorithms. Since our search only produced one hit, our search engine does not have to rank the results. Ranking algorithms, however, are where actual Web search engines tend to vary the most, since there are so many possible factors by which to compare each document; these algorithms are addressed in the next part of this chapter.

Recall that our example query included a Boolean **AND** operator, which required that all of the pages retrieved contain **Australia** and at least one of the other keywords. Some search tools do not offer Boolean searching. Instead, their search engines use a complicated set of ranking algorithms to produce a large, but well-ordered set of results. For example, a natural language approach might ignore the **AND** in our query. Rather than retrieving only pages with two or more of the three keywords, it would retrieve every page that contained *any one or more* of the keywords; however, its ranking process would move every page containing all three words to the top of the list, followed by every page containing two, then every page containing one of the query terms. Thus the non-Boolean search engine would retrieve a larger set of pages than ours for the same query, but it would present the same results as ours—ahead of the rest. The assumption is that users would prefer to see pages containing all of their query keywords first, regardless of whether their search was broad or narrow, while having the option of looking at a more complete set.

While our search engine does read Boolean syntax, it also uses a process like the one described above to present the results that it retrieves in ranked order. If we replace the **AND** operator with **OR** in our example query, changing it to

Australia* or www or au

we retrieve two hits, since both of the pages in our index contain at least one of the keywords. Now that there is more than one hit in the results, our engine has something to rank. Our ranking algorithms act on the same principles as the natural language query engine described above. The engine generates a temporary table:

Address	Number of Keywords Found	Number of Times Each Keyword Appears	Fields Where Keywords Occur
www.webawards.info.au	2	1,1	Title,URL
www.weightwatchers.com	1	1	URL

Since the Awards page contains two of the query words (remember that our search engine does not recognize **au** as a word), it ranks higher than the Weight Watchers page, which only contains one term. Thus our results will present the Awards page ahead of the Weight Watchers page.

RANKING ALGORITHMS

Ranking algorithms consider features other than which and how many query words occur in each page, in order to achieve finer measures of relative worth among search results. Some search engines factor the particular fields, such as the <TITLE> and URL, in which query terms occur into the ranking process. Similarly, how close to the beginning of the document a keyword appears, as well as how many times that keyword appears in a single document, may be factored into the ranking process.

Some engines consider the order in which words appear in the query. In our example, this would mean that a document containing three instances of the word **Australia** and one of **www** would rank higher than a document containing the converse. Many ranking algorithms consider the length of the Web page, giving greater weight to words in shorter documents. In our case, this would mean that a short document with two occurrences of **Australia** would rank higher than a long document with the same number of occurrences. The reasoning here is that since **Australia** represents a greater percentage of the *text* of a short document, it will represent a proportionately greater percentage of the *content*.

Ranking algorithms convert all of these factors into numerical weights for each query word or phrase. They combine these numbers with the statistical measures of the Web pages to produce a single score for each page in the results set. The pages are presented to the user in descending order by these scores. Some search tools include the raw score with the summary as part of the user's display, while other tools normalize the scores to a percentage between 0 and 100, or omit the scores entirely.

There are pros and cons to every method of searching and ranking. Many search tools are designed based on the premise that Boolean language is too archaic and complicated for most of their users; instead these tools provide the opportunity to search with natural language techniques. Boolean queries are certainly inappropriate for some users, especially novice searchers. Many searchers routinely use natural language queries even when such queries are not supported; they reasonably (but mistakenly) assume that a machine can be questioned like a reference librarian. On the other hand, automatic indexing—even with recent advances—is still in its infancy. Experienced searchers will rarely want to give up control of the search process to the "man behind the curtain," especially when Web search tools provide the user with so little information as to how their indexes are built and searched.

Further, every method of statistically ranking documents is only useful in certain contexts. Each of the approaches we have mentioned could present the same set of results in an entirely different order. This is one reason that the same search often produces quite different results with different search tools. This also means that the Help or FAQ information provided for a specific search tool can be misleading or uninformative. A typical description of the ranking algorithm for a search tool in a Help file might read, "SuperSearch gives you the best results first by ranking them based on YOUR search terms!" Although this description is accurate for all of the variations discussed above, it is not very informative. Specific details are rarely available. Users beware.

Chapter 4

The Interface

Users never really come into direct contact with any of the parts of Web search tools that we have discussed so far. Robots, indexes, databases, and search engines all live and operate on the server, perhaps a continent away from the user's PC client. The interface is the part of the search tool with which users directly interact. The interface is what the user sees, hears, and manipulates. It is the medium of communication between the user and the search engine. The interface prompts the user and interprets for the user the search engine's abilities. It provides the place for entering a query, then prompts the search engine and translates the user's query (with varying degrees of skill) into the engine's language and potential actions. From here the engine searches the index and reports back its findings. The interface presents the results to the user in one of a variety of possible formats.

Since the user interface is the only part of the search tool that the user sees, it can appear to be *the* defining part. It dictates what the user may type and what results appear on screen. This can make it hard to think of WebCrawler, HotBot, or any other search tool as something other than what appears on screen. Yet, although this is a crucial part of the tool, it is also the most malleable and thus the most subject to change. To illustrate, having sat down one Saturday and taken notes on which to base a description of the WebCrawler interface, we found the following Saturday that both the look and possible query types had been substantially revised. Certain choices of search types had been eliminated, others had been added, the structure and content of descriptive and Help pages had been modified, and a number of auxiliary links and features added.

From the perspective of the creators of a Web search tool, the user interface is the simplest component. The creation and maintenance of indexes and search-and-retrieval software consumes far more time and resources than the series of Web pages and simple CGI (Common Gateway Interface) scripts that the search tool contributes to the interface. The interface is far more complicated, however, than the server's end of things implies; it ultimately plays as large a role in the effective retrieval of information as any of the other components we have discussed.

The user interface is composed of several parts. As we mentioned, the search tool provides a set of one or more HTML pages, which are what the user actually sees on the screen. The appearance of these pages is largely determined by the browser, however. Browsers, such as Netscape Navigator, Microsoft Explorer, Lynx, and Mosaic, read and interpret the HTML code of the Web pages. They decide how this information will be displayed to the user. For example, depending on the user's browser, a search tool's home page could appear as animated pictures, color, and text; static color images and text; colored text; or plain black-and-white ASCII text. A more radical problem arises when the user's browser cannot interact with forms, the means by which most search tools transmit the user's search request from the PC to the server. Like the browser, the user's hardware and other software all play a role in determining how the interface appears to the user.

Cookies.txt

Cookies.txt is a file stored in the Netscape directory of the user's PC. The Netscape browser uses the file to store user preferences, such as passwords and favorite formats. Some Web search tools use cookies.txt to store information about past sessions. Their server retrieves these records at the beginning of each interaction with a user on that PC. For example, when a HotBot user creates a customized interface, HotBot saves the information in the cookies.txt file. Excite offers a similar feature. So far (as of early 1997) we have not detected any other uses of the cookies.txt file by Web search tools, but the potential exists for them to target advertising by recording demographic data and the subjects of user interest from past searches. The following is an example of a "cookie" from a cookies.txt file:

    www.business.com FALSE / FALSE 942191940 IAF 1c88a

It gives the coded user preferences for accessing the www.business.com site. Netscape currently limits the cookies.txt file to 300 cookies, each less than 300 K, and with no more than 20 cookies from one server.

The interface ultimately defines the set of potential user queries, in the same way that the search engine defines the set of possible searches and the index defines the available information. The search engine may be able to perform a certain type of search, but if the interface provides no way for the user to request that search, it will never happen. Similarly, if the search tool provides poor Help documents or FAQs, the user will not know how to exploit the search options fully. The user can only do what the interface allows.

ENTERING A SEARCH

Most interactions between users and search tools center around one or more command lines. The command line is usually a box near the center of the initial screen of the home page. Clicking on the box brings up a cursor in the command line. Users may enter keywords or natural language phrases in the command line, and then submit the query by clicking a nearby button.

Some interfaces let the user include traditional Boolean operators in the command line. Operators like *AND*, *OR*, *NOT*, and *NEAR* connect keywords to form a search statement, or query. The browser submits the search statement to the server, where the search engine transforms it and compares it to the index. Some search tools offer symbols (for example, +, −, /, &) in place of word operators. Recalling our earlier example (a search for documents containing *Australia** and either *www* or **au**), different user interfaces might require very different formats for the same search of the same database, even with the same search engine. Possibilities include

```
+Australia* +(www / au)
```
[Search]

```
+Australia* +(www / au)
```
[Search]

```
+Australia* www au
```
[Search]

```
Australia Australian Australians www au
```
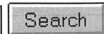 [Search]

Each interface can offer its own combination of operators, symbols, and punctuation marks (or lack thereof) independent of the index and search engine. Users must pay attention and routinely look for the appropriate syntax for the interface to a new search tool. Sometimes the same syntax carries different meanings in different tools. Even a familiar tool may change its interface overnight.

Some interfaces allow natural language phrases, instead of, or in addition to, Boolean options. In these cases, the user types a question, phrase, or any list of words. The interface submits the query as a whole and the search engine pulls out certain keywords and performs the search. For example

Who was the first President of the United States?

is a natural language query. Users must be careful in crafting natural language queries, contrary to the boasts of the search tools that offer it. Recall that many search tools do not index some traditional stopwords. Some of the most common stopwords are question words, such as *why*, *who*, *what*, *where*, and *how*. Natural language query tools often encourage users to submit search statements in the form of a question, even though the search engine may ignore the question words. Frequently these tools pluck the keywords from the query and compare them against the index, just as in a Boolean search statement. The job of moving the best hits to the top falls on the statistical ranking algorithms.

In our example, the user would have retrieved the same results if the search statement had been

```
first President United States          | Search |
```

The fact that the search was in the form of a question had no impact. In fact no search tool currently available can understand the difference between **Where is George Washington** and **Who is George Washington**.

Still other interfaces offer more than one command box for a single search. In one approach, the user must type each word of the search statement into its own box; from a menu, the user chooses operators to connect the boxes. In addition, there may be special boxes and menus for such limits as date ranges and file formats. Similar boxes may look for contents only in specific fields, such as Title and URL. Once the user fills in all of the appropriate boxes on the screen, the entire form is submitted to the search engine.

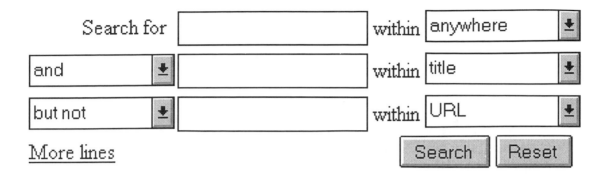

RESULTS

The query page of the interface is a static file created beforehand and accessed over and over by thousands of users for millions of searches. Even in interactive pages to which the user can add or delete extra command lines, the interface is a standard shell—the same home page at a fixed address for every user who wanders by. Every user needs a starting point, and the starting point has to be prepared for any user. On the other hand, since the search tool cannot know the content and order of the search results before a search is submitted, there is no fixed page for the user to view the results. To display the search results, the search tool creates new temporary pages on the fly, by plugging the search results into a template of HTML codes.

The user's custom results page is typically a set of citations, each composed of, at minimum, a hypertext link in the form of a Title or URL. This link is to the named page itself, not to a copy of the page in the search tool's databases. This is an extremely important point to remember when using and evaluating Web search tools. Even though the user is searching the search tool's index, the results are links to the Web. Thus, if a page linked to the results has been moved or deleted, or if its home server is unavailable or too busy, or if any of a number of other mishaps has occurred, the user may not be able to reach the page. A dead link is all but useless.

Unlike self-contained online commercial databases, the results from Web searches are pointers to locations that, at some point in the past, actually held a particular document. These pointers rarely contain any useful information in and of themselves—their value depends on whether or not they actually lead the user to the associated document. In contrast, an online database such as MEDLINE contains directly useful information in the search results. Although the most important information is the citation, which leads the user to the full document, citations to journal or monographic literature are not dependent on the user's access to a particular copy of the item. Even if a local issue of the *New England Journal of Medicine* is missing, the citation information from the MEDLINE search is enough to request the document through interlibrary loan. Although a library catalog is focused directly on a given collection of documents, it too provides the searcher with enough information to access the cited material through other means (such as by ordering the book from the publisher or buying it at a bookstore).

If a link in the results of a Web search does not actually retrieve its associated document, the information is all but useless, even if the missing document was relevant to the search. Links usually fail because the page referenced is no longer at its old address. The author or webmaster may have deleted the page or simply may have given it a new URL. Either way, the old URL is no longer useful information. Even if the missing page is duplicated elsewhere on the Web, the information in the results list may not point the user to the document. In some cases, if the missing document has a title, or if an automatic summary with useful text accompanies the dead link, the user can attempt to search for it with this information using another Web search tool. Yet even in these cases, the missing document would still have to be available on some Web server, and the second search tool would have to have indexed the document at its new URL.

The moral is that the number, quality, and ranking of the hits in the search results is not an accurate measure of the tool's worth to the user. A useful Web search must produce active links to relevant documents.

Most Web search tools return the results to the user in groups of ten hits. Some tools simply retrieve a title or URL, but most provide at least the option of viewing an automatically generated summary. The results appear in ranked order, from highest to lowest score. Users scroll down the page to view hits lower on the list. When the user finishes examining each set of ten hits, he or she may click a button to request another set of hits. When this happens, the search tool creates another temporary Web page containing a new set of ten hits. Most search tools only allow the user to proceed through the sets of ten in linear order: numbers 1–10, then 11–20, then 21–30, and so on. A few offer ways (such as a row of hotlinked numbers, each representing a group of ten links) to jump around among the sets.

HELP

Ideally, Help documents explain the syntax and features of a search tool. But most search tools have lousy Help files (which comes as no surprise to anyone familiar with online Help in other contexts). Ironically, few users ever access Help documentation to begin with, so this crime frequently has no victims. Nevertheless, anyone who uses a Web search tool for any important searches should get into the habit of checking available Help. In particular, users should look for information about available operators (such as **AND**, **OR**, **+**, **–**), options for how results are ranked, and defaults for how the tool interprets searches (such as automatically treating two words as a phrase, rather than separate keywords).

One of the main problems with Help documentation in the tools we review is that the Help authors frequently seem unfamiliar with the tool. As Web search tools become part of large corporations, the responsibilities for different facets of their design fall on distributed groups and individuals. Sometimes the Help documentation falls into the hands of the marketing or public relations department, far removed from the creators and developers, and it turns into an advertisement, with predictable inaccuracy. We check any claims and features mentioned in the Help documentation whenever we evaluate a tool. On several occasions, even the Help examples provided to illustrate a feature have not worked! This often happens when the interface or search engine is replaced with a new model, but someone forgot to remove the old Help files describing old features.

In other cases, the Help information is accurate—even detailed—but terribly organized. A common format for Help information is the FAQ list. This is simply a list of canned questions and answers, which make it look like the search tool is diligently answering its mail. In fact, most questions are crafted around the answers that the tool is prepared to provide, rather than the other way around. FAQ questions are rarely in any sort of order, thus forcing users to scroll through them until they find a useful nugget—a rather primitive approach for a tool designed to retrieve information.

Good Help files (they do exist) usually center around examples of how to construct a query (especially how to fix a bad one), with careful descriptions of the process of retrieving and evaluating results. An even better Help file would describe both how the index is built and what the search tool's shortcomings are—none that we have encountered so far includes such a feature. One of the problems with the increasingly commercial nature of Web search tools is finding an altogether honest one. It simply is not good advertising to talk about what your product does poorly or not at all. Users should always check the Help files, then try to verify what they say.

The rest of the interface can be populated by a wide variety of features, from links to Web page reviews to searchable databases of road maps. Most Web search tools now sell third-party advertising. Typically about one quarter of the user's screen (usually the top) will display a wide banner ad linked to a corporate or consumer product home page on the Web. Some ads are static images, while others flicker and move. Although ads can be intrusive (especially Java tornados!), they are an admittedly minor annoyance to endure for free searches.

Ultimately, any good interface offers ease of use and clear communication. Search options should be briefly described with examples, features should be clearly labeled, and everything even remotely important to a search should be easily accessible from the first screen of the home page.

SECTION III

UNDERSTANDING AND USING SEVEN SEARCH ENGINES

Chapter 5

Introduction to the Search Engines, and Nine General Searching Tips

The number and kind of search tools on the Internet changes daily. Hundreds of search tools are available on the Web. In addition, existing search tool appearances, options, and features change constantly. We used the following criteria to decide which tools to evaluate for this book:

1. **Each search tool must be widely known and used**. We judged satisfaction of this criterion by tracking several search engine listings on the Internet, especially on Yahoo!'s *Searching the Web* pages,[1] the *All-in-One* page,[2] and Netscape's *Global Search* page.[3] All of the engines that we investigated are (or were) listed on all these pages. We also checked periodicals for reviews and discussions.[4]

2. **Each search tool must incorporate a robot-generated index, with little or no human involvement in the indexing process.** We wanted to examine the automatic aspects of Web search and retrieval, not argue about the subject classification choices of an individual tool. This criterion excluded many of the most popular sites, such as Yahoo! and the Clearinghouse for Subject-Oriented Resource Guides, which we use extensively ourselves. Robot-generated indexes provide the closest thing to a comprehensive index of the Web currently available.

3. **Each search tool's index must cover any category of information from all parts of the Web.** This criterion does not mean that we required a comprehensive search tool, especially since there is not one. We wanted to examine general interest indexes, not subject- or format-specific ones. All of the tools we discuss use robots that will retrieve any Web document they encounter, no matter what its subject or origin is. Again, this criterion ex-

cluded many of the best sites on the Web. If the database only included a narrow format (like WhoWhere's e-mail addresses) or only searched for one subject (like the English Server at Carnegie Mellon Univeristy) we did not consider it.

4. **Each search tool must offer user searches free of charge.** To make this book as useful as possible, we only evaluated free, general interest search tools.

The criteria for examining the engines themselves was a little more complicated. We initially wanted to compare the search engines and rank them by their results for specific queries, but differences in style among the tools made this impossible. Some accept only Boolean-structured search statements, while others accept only natural-language queries or lists of keywords. Some tools offer both "advanced" and "simple" searches. Others offer combinations of all these variables. None of them offers the same combination of keyword operators. These and other variations convinced us that we could not even consistently duplicate search statements across sites. Further, the size and chaotic behavior of the Web meant that we had no reliable data from which to calculate recall and precision figures, nor could we take a static snapshot of the Web and search all of the tools simultaneously. It would have been unfair to readers and to the search tools to pretend that we could accurately obtain and compare statistical and relevancy data.

Both print and online review literature frequently rank search tools based on speed, number of hits, and other objective data. We started to follow this path, but quickly found that most Web search engines now produce search results in a matter of seconds. In addition, from the user's position, Internet traffic, local connection speed, and other factors beyond a search tool's control largely govern retrieval time. As for results, all of the sites we covered routinely produce hundreds of times as many hits as any user could ever wade through. The strengths and weaknesses of a search tool's ranking process, which can push the best 20 hits out of 200,000 to the top of the list or leave them scattered at random, are far more important to know. Since this is far more difficult to measure objectively, our interest drifted more toward a subjective evaluation based on our own satisfaction *as users* over time.

We decided to concentrate on the individual usefulness of each search tool from the perspective of different sorts of users. We are three very different users, and we each used and evaluated all of the search tools in this book. To broaden our scope, we each tried to play a variety of roles. We used different types of queries, trying to emulate novice and experienced online searchers with various information needs and environments. We considered a variety of possible user desires for search results (for example, broad versus narrow, subject specificity, large versus small sets). Questions like "Did we have to follow too many links to get an answer to our question?" or "How hard was it to create a good query?" or "Were there too many dead links in the results?" would receive different answers from different users, but they are the most important types of questions users should ask about Web search tools. Our results, then, realistically relate what it is like to use and evaluate these tools.[5]

Chapters 6–12 explain how each search tool works. We describe how to use each tool's simple and sophisticated search capabilities, discuss which commands and operators are available on which engine, and do a little detective (and guess) work to illuminate how each tool builds and searches its index. Some of this information is not available in FAQs, and sometimes we contradict what a search tool says about itself. We tested any claims and examples in a search tool's documentation before we repeated them here. Whenever possible we contacted the companies to try to clear up mysteries and apparent inconsistencies, although the companies were by far our least productive resource.

Search tools are always changing how they look and what they offer; therefore we have focused on those characteristics that are least likely to change frequently. Our aim is to help readers understand the inner workings of Web search tools enough to exploit and evaluate them for some time to come, despite their inevitable changes.

TIPS

Searching the Web can be as easy as picking a search tool, typing a word or two, pressing enter, and selecting the first page that appears on the results list. For some purposes, this technique works fairly well. For instance, if users are just out to surf for fun, they may require little from the starting point. However, anyone with high standards for search results (such as a librarian searching on behalf of a patron, or a researcher exploring the literature in his or her field on the Web) needs to know how best to exploit the available tools. Chapters 6–12 offer our reviews and reports of a number of the major tools that index the Web. We preface these chapters with the following tips that we hope will ease the frustration of searching the Web and increase the likelihood of finding useful results.

Tip 1: Have a Good Vocabulary

No matter what the topic or the search tool is, the user should be armed with a good vocabulary. Information on the Web originates from authors of every age, nationality, background, and educational level. Thus, even for the simplest topic, the user should search with carefully chosen keywords. Always consider synonyms (for example, clinical studies may use *neoplasm* or *carcinoma*, whereas consumer health pamphlets may use *cancer* when discussing the same concepts), antonyms (for example, a good way to find pages devoted to peace studies is to search for *war* or *violence*, common topics in the field), homonyms (for example, *book* refers to a monograph or to the act of scheduling something, depending on the context), variant spellings and foreign terms (such as *color* and *colour*), and variant word forms and plurals (such as *write writing*, and *written*; *mouse* and *mice*). This does not mean that every search should contain all of these types of words. In fact, some search engines automatically try to account for some of these problems themselves (for example, by automatically truncating words in the user's query to retrieve plurals). But users should remember that, while successful searching requires the appropriate choice of terminology, the Web offers no controlled vocabulary or subject headings.

Tip 2: Use Boolean Searches

Not every search tool on the Web offers traditional Boolean query syntax. However, most do offer it in some form, and it is still the most powerful and ubiquitous method for constructing queries in other types of online databases. There are three common Boolean operators: *AND*, *OR*, and *NOT*. Together with two or more keywords, these operators tell a search engine to assemble groups, or *sets*, of pages with common features. These common features are determined by the user's query. For example,

   dogs and cats

tells the search engine to assemble the set of pages that contain the word *dogs* and a second set of pages containing the word *cats*. These sets are represented by circles below.

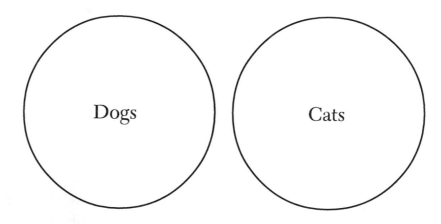

The *AND* operator signals the search engine to create a third set of pages, each member of which contains both *dogs* and *cats*. The search engine compares the two previous sets, identifies any pages that occur in both, and assembles these pages into the results set for the user. We illustrate this below by joining the two circles. The shaded area where the circles overlap represents the results, that is, those Web pages that reside in both sets, in the shared space.

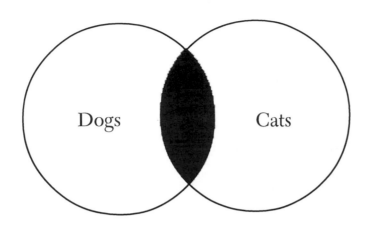

In the search statement

dogs or cats

the **OR** operator tells the search engine to combine the two sets. This union creates a superset containing all of the members of both sets. Some of the pages will contain only the word **dogs**; some will contain only the word **cats**; the rest will contain both words. We illustrate this by shading in the entire area of both sets:

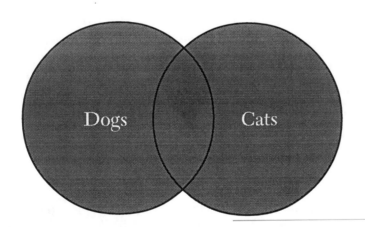

The **NOT** operator tells the search engine to create a set of pages containing the word to its left, none of which contain the word to its right. Thus, the search

dogs not cats

would create a set of pages containing the word **dogs**, but not the word **cats**. We illustrate this by shading in the area of the **dogs** set that does not overlap the **cats** set:

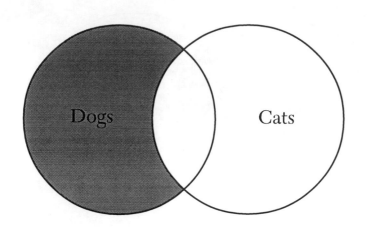

Keep in mind that connecting terms with **OR** almost always produces many more hits than connecting them with **AND**. The **OR** search will retrieve everything that the **AND** search retrieves, plus everything the **NOT** search retrieves, plus some that neither of these would find.

The **NOT** operator should be used with great care. If you are interested in every page about dogs, but you specifically do not want pages on cats, the search

dogs not cats

would not be a good approach. There will definitely be pages on the Web that are exclusively devoted to dogs, but that contain the word **cats**. If a page were titled *All About Dogs (But Nothing About Cats)*, it would not be retrieved by the above search—even if the word **cats** never appears in it anywhere else. On the other hand, the search would retrieve the page titled *Everything About Felines (But Nothing About Dogs)*, which only refers to cats as **felines**. The **NOT** operator can radically reduce the size of the sets you retrieve, but usually at the cost of some relevant information.

Tip 3: Check the Syntax

Know the basic syntax and defaults of the search tool. If the tool requires Boolean language the user will need to create a very different search statement from that if the tool will not allow it. Some tools allow the user to enter both natural language and Boolean queries. Often the difference is that the search engine actually ignores the Boolean operators, although it will search for the keywords in a Boolean query by default. The user may think that the Boolean language is working, when in fact it is not—a simple list of keywords would have retrieved the same results. The user needs to know how the tool interprets a search statement. The first place to look is in the Help or FAQ files, or in a book such as this one. Other than that, try using various search strategies and comparing the results to see if the search tool treats them differently.

Tip 4: Check for Stopwords

Be aware of stopwords (some indexes have them, others do not, and no two indexes use exactly the same ones) and special character restrictions (some search engines will not look for numerals, punctuation marks, or other nonalphabetic characters).

Tip 5: Never Stop with One

Never stop after just one search. Unless you are looking for a specific page or fact and find it on the first attempt, try several permutations of your search strategy. Almost any change in the structure or vocabulary of a search statement will change the results, either by finding different pages or reranking the original hits. It only takes an extra minute or two to perform several searches, and you will gain a much better feel for the available resources and search options. When practical, keep a log of the terms and strategies you use on each tool. This can make it surprisingly easy to compare the search tools after the fact, and prevents needless backtracking. As you find good pages in your search results, bookmark them in a temporary subdirectory—this allows you to continue trying new search strategies and different search tools, while keeping a growing set of the best results. Also, each search tool has its own database of Web pages that will retrieve different results for the same search. Try to use at least two different tools for any search.

Tip 6: Avoid Meta-Tools

Although we recommend that you never stop after searching with just one Web search tool, we also recommend that you avoid Web sites that search multiple tools for you. Quite a few sites allow the user to type in a search, then submit that search to several Web engines at once. So for example, you could search for **dogs and cats** and simultaneously receive results from AltaVista, Excite, OpenText, and Infoseek. This may appear to be a perfect solution, but it is not. We hope that the following chapters will make it very clear that every search tool interprets queries differently. Some offer Boolean searching, some do not. Some Boolean engines use word operators (like **AND**), some use symbols (like **+**) instead. Some automatically truncate the words in the user query, some do not. None of the meta-search sites linked to multiple search tools circumvents all of these differences. The user is almost invariably much better off searching each tool separately.

Tip 7: Avoid Date Searches

Avoid date searches on the Web, including keyword searches limited by dates. Some Web search tools will not retrieve dates or numerals. Those that do rarely specify what date is being searched (the date a page was first posted? the date it was last updated? the date it was harvested? copyrighted?). If the search is limited by a range of dates, what happens to pages with no date attached to them (excluding the date of harvest)? The user is rarely able to answer these questions.

Tip 8: Be Cautious

It is more difficult to authenticate information from the Web than from traditional resources. Anyone can put a page on the Web. Out-of-date information may or may not be removed or updated, and there are often no publication or copyright dates to establish currency. In the print world, the accuracy of published information is usually the responsibility of the author, editor, and reviewers. On the Web, frequently only the author is responsible. For good or ill, this must be borne in mind.

Tip 9: Use a Variety of Tools

Remember that Web robots do not harvest the contents of databases linked to the Web. For example, imagine a library with a Web page through which users can search its online catalog. Although a robot will harvest the library's Web page, it cannot harvest the contents of the catalog. Similarly, even though many Web sites allow you to search ERIC, none of the general Web search tools that harvest those sites can index the contents of the ERIC database. General Web search tools can only take you to the pages from which you may search such databases as ERIC.

Always remember that few of the available Web search tools are interested in sending you to a competitor. Even though your searches are free, you are a desirable consumer of advertising. Search tools can boast like carnival barkers, but inflated claims should be of no consequence to a perceptive user.

NOTES

1.   http://www.yahoo.com/
2.   http://www.albany.net/allinone/
3.   http://home.netscape.com/escapes/search/global_search.html
4.   Primary print sources include *PC Magazine, Info World, Internet Guide,* and other news-oriented computer periodicals.
5.   See the appendix for evaluative criteria.

Chapter 6

WebCrawler

http://www.webcrawler.com

HISTORY

Although WebCrawler only began in early 1994, the rapid obsolescence in the Web environment makes WebCrawler something of a grandfatherly figure. For now WebCrawler is the official Web search engine for America Online (AOL). Although AOL is a subscription-based service, it has continued to allow free use of WebCrawler by any Web user. Further, AOL claims that WebCrawler will remain freely available to all for the foreseeable future. Although this may be the case, WebCrawler's increasingly geriatric status coupled with the fee-based services' frenzied scrambles to attract customers may force WebCrawler's stay with AOL to be brief. For now, though, WebCrawler is still one of the simplest and most accessible search tools available.

WebCrawler was created by Brian Pinkerton as a research project at the University of Washington in Seattle. Increasingly frustrated with the serendipitous *surfing* approach to retrieving information on the Web, Pinkerton sought to develop an *agent* that would collect Web pages automatically, based on a predefined algorithm, and order them into an index that he could search at his leisure. Now frequently referred to as *robots*, his agents provided a way to sample broad swaths of the Web in varying degrees of depth without constant human intervention. The information and links that were returned could be stored and indexed for flexible searching at any later time. Even more, the agents would use their past results to direct future searches, placing some control over the problem of duplicate results and taking advantage of the human effort embodied in the established links between Web pages.

HOW WEBCRAWLER ADDS DOCUMENTS TO ITS DATABASE

Discovery robots travel the Web gathering the URLs of active pages and compiling them into a database. WebCrawler's harvester searches the Web for new information to add to its index by dipping into this pool of URLs and choosing one as its starting point. The database contains URLs for new pages that WebCrawler has never indexed and those that it has harvested before. If the page has been indexed, WebCrawler's large keyword index also contains the text from the body of the page. The harvester indexes such pages again to update any changes in their content.

WebCrawler guides its robots' behavior with two different strategies. In the broader of the two search strategies, WebCrawler sends the robots to fetch the oldest unvisited pages whose URLs it has accumulated. The robot retrieves the specific document associated with the URL via CERN's WWW library, then integrates the text into WebCrawler's publicly searchable index. The harvester then turns around and chooses the next oldest URL, unrelated to the previous page, and repeats the process. WebCrawler uses a similar strategy to decide which pages in its index to update, beginning with the oldest and moving forward.

In the narrower strategy, WebCrawler searches its own index for a page that it judges relevant to a specific topic, rather than searching the oldest pages of the broader search. WebCrawler dispatches a robot to gather new pages and links from the (presumably) relevant document, on the assumption that links attached to a document (either by persons or automatic means) will lead to other documents that have a useful subject overlap with the initial one. This is a directed search, which actually searches the Web for specific types of new documents based on their subject. WebCrawler can use this approach to fill specific gaps in its subject coverage.

The differences between these two approaches are in which documents the robot chooses as the starting point, and how "deeply" the robot follows links outward from that document before backing up and starting all over again. As we mentioned in Chapter 2, one of the problems with robots in the Web environment is that their rapid, repeated requests can cause considerable trouble for individual Web servers. At best these requests slow server operations, at worst they can crash the server. In response to this problem, WebCrawler's broad search does not seek to follow links from the document it first retrieves. Rather, it is an abrupt search that, following its initial retrieval, goes back to the pool of old documents in the database to find another document and start over. The reasoning is that it is assumed that documents are likely to be most heavily linked to other documents on the same site/server. If one considers the prevalence of help links on search engine pages or the nesting of departmental pages within a university site as examples, it is easy to see that a robot could put considerable strain on a particular site in attempting to follow all of the links from a single page, and the resulting links from each of these. WebCrawler therefore takes a comparatively random approach in its broad searches in order to avoid this situation. It tries to ask for as little as possible each time it visits a server.

In its narrower searches, WebCrawler is not so thoughtful, although its does take measures to reduce the strain it causes. Given the above premise that narrower, more specific searches should follow the links of an initial relevant document, it is not possible for the narrow search to proceed with the same care for its hosts. To offset this, WebCrawler restricts the frequency of its requests to a single server to one per minute. It also places an upper bound on the total number of documents a search can retrieve from a single server. This may produce a trade-off in search success, abandoning some relevant documents before they are reached and retrieving more slowly than WebCrawler is capable, but it maintains good will between the server and WebCrawler.

WebCrawler is constantly harvesting new pages in these ways. It claims to update its index daily. Beyond these automatic means of gathering information, WebCrawler encourages authors to submit the URLs of their pages, rather than wait for the robots to discover them (or not).

INTERFACE AND SEARCHING

Until April 1996 WebCrawler employed one of the easiest, yet least powerful search interfaces on the Web. It consisted of a single command line into which the user could type any combination of words, either like a shopping list of terms or natural language queries such as sentences. Having done so, the user could choose to have the search conjoin all of the terms (essentially connecting them with Boolean *AND*) or search for any occurrence of any combination of them (that is, connecting all words with Boolean *OR*). The pages retrieved in the first case would each contain all of the search words. In the second case, each page would contain at least one of the search words (although the order in which the results were presented dictated that pages with the highest number of term occurrences relative to total number of words would appear first). Punctuation (for example, parentheses) was ignored, effectively eliminating further Boolean sophistication in query formation.

Webcrawler's current search interface and engine are considerably improved, however, moving WebCrawler closer to the look and feel of its competitors. The single command line remains, but the variety of search forms available within it has changed markedly. The menu choice of *AND*ing or *OR*ing all of the query words is gone. If the user enters a natural language statement or a simple list of search terms, WebCrawler connects all of the terms with Boolean *OR* by default, thus searching for any combination of the terms within a Web page. WebCrawler then ranks the results so that those pages containing all or most of the terms appear first, followed by the rest of the pages, each in succession containing fewer and fewer of the user's search terms. Pull-down menus below the command line allow the user to specify the format of the search results. Results can be requested in groups of 10, 25, or 100 and in the form of one-line titles or summaries.

The net change in simple searches from the old interface is that one does not have the option of preventing the return of pages that contain fewer than all of the search terms. For novice or impatient users, this makes a simple interface even simpler, without sacrificing any results. A lack of choices is often a very pleasing sight in the Web environment. Since many users are prone to skip the instructions and drop-down windows that adorn many interfaces, the predetermined nature of WebCrawler's simple search likely prevents many unintended results sets that would occur with user searches of some other Web search tools. The novice user must acquire a little more knowledge, however, and type a few more characters, to bring back a smaller, tighter results set. Such refinement is possible because of the Boolean and linguistic operators that are now available in WebCrawler's advanced search option.

Users create advanced searches on WebCrawler within the same single command line as simple searches. The user determines the advanced character of the search by including operators and punctuation between search terms. Users may employ the three standard Boolean operators (*AND*, *OR*, and *NOT*), as well as *NEAR* and *ADJ*, which restrict search results to pages containing occurrences of terms within specified distances of one another or in a particular order. For example

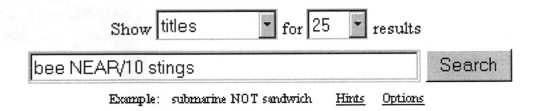

would retrieve pages with the word *bee* appearing within ten words on either side of the word *stings*. On the other hand, would only retrieve pages containing the phrase ***bee stings***—it would not retrieve the phrase ***stings bee***.

The user's available punctuation consists of parentheses and quotation marks. Parentheses determine the order in which WebCrawler processes the operators in the query— they define the bounds within which the operators operate. For example,

Show [titles ▾] for [25 ▾] results

[bees AND (stings or hives)]   [Search]

Example: submarine NOT sandwich   Hints   Options

tells WebCrawler to search for pages containing the word ***bee*** and one of the other words, ***stings*** or ***hives***. WebCrawler would also retrieve any pages containing all three words, since such pages also meet the criteria of containing ***bee*** and one of the other words. (In fact, given how WebCrawler ranks results to determine the order of presentation, pages with all three words would appear ahead of the others.) Quotation marks define phrases in a search. Thus

Show [titles ▾] for [25 ▾] results

["bee stings"]   [Search]

Example: submarine NOT sandwich   Hints   Options

would retrieve pages with that exact phrase. This is essentially a shortcut to using ***NEAR*** and ***ADJ***, since

Show [titles ▾] for [25 ▾] results

[bees ADJ stings]   [Search]

Example: submarine NOT sandwich   Hints   Options

would return the same pages, as would

(bee NEAR stings) NOT ((stings ADJ bee) NOT (bee ADJ stings)).

When the user includes only one set of parentheses or quotation marks, he or she may omit the closing parenthesis or quotation mark without consequence. This renders the following two search statements identical:

Show titles ▾ for 25 ▾ results

bees AND (stings or hives)   Search

Example: submarine NOT sandwich   Hints   Options

Show titles ▾ for 25 ▾ results

bee AND (stings OR hives   Search

Example: submarine NOT sandwich   Hints   Options

as well as these:

Show titles ▾ for 25 ▾ results

"bee stings"   Search

Example: submarine NOT sandwich   Hints   Options

Show titles ▾ for 25 ▾ results

"bee stings   Search

Example: submarine NOT sandwich   Hints   Options

The most confusing aspect of WebCrawler's query interface is also that which makes it simple. Since both the simple/natural language queries and the advanced/ Boolean queries must be entered on the same command line (and there is no button to click or other mechanism to "turn on" an advanced query mode), a user whose natural language query contains the words *AND*, *OR*, *NOT*, or *NEAR*, or uses parentheses or quotation marks, will not necessarily get what he or she expects. For one, natural language relies more on context and inflection than parentheses to indicate the scope and intention of operative words such as those within a statement. Further, natural language tends to give the words **AND** and **OR** the opposite meanings of their Boolean definitions.

To illustrate, the natural language query

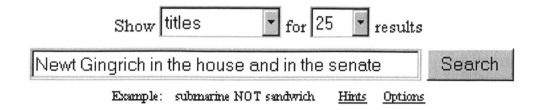

probably means that the user would like information about Newt Gingrich in connection with the Senate or in connection with the House, or both. On the other hand, the Boolean formation of this query would require something like

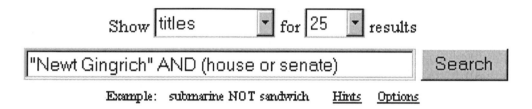

If the query had not included **AND**, all of the terms would have been automatically connected by **OR**, creating a set including all of the possible results from our Boolean interpretation, plus many others. But the presence of the **and** in the natural language query signals to WebCrawler that all of the documents must include the word **senate**. Since Newt is Speaker of the House of Representatives, and not a senator, this will omit at least some pages that deal with him and his job (and are thus quite relevant to the user's need), simply because they have no mention of the Senate.

Another WebCrawler default relevant to natural language queries is stopwords. WebCrawler ignores a set of common words that fail to indicate subject content. In the previous natural language query

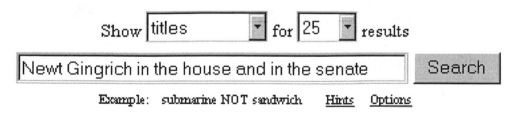

the search engine would ignore the words **on**, **in**, and **the**, resulting in the actual search query

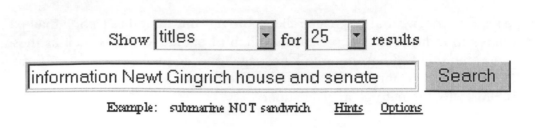

Given the defaults, this search would be equivalent to the Boolean form

(information OR Newt OR Gingrich OR house) AND senate.

Unfortunately, WebCrawler does not provide a list of its stopwords. It claims to add words automatically to its stop list once it decides they have passed some threshold of occurrences as compared to most other words on the Web. In this way it presumably omits words that clearly do occur too frequently on the Web, rather than just using common practice to choose the stopwords. This feature can also create strange situations, however, such as the fact that WebCrawler will search for the word **why**, but not the word **when**, since the former has passed the threshold while the other has not. It is unclear why the list is hidden from the user.

WebCrawler does not offer truncation. User searches must include plurals, variant spellings, and various word forms to retrieve comprehensive results. Thus, to search for all Web pages with some variant of **jog**, the user must create a query like

jog OR jogging OR jogger OR joggers OR jogged OR jogs

In addition to user searches, WebCrawler offers a small set of broad subject links to reviews of pages that its human operators have deemed *Best of the Net*. Users may browse the hierarchical structure of subject links to find exceptional pages, but the set of reviewed pages is too small to satisfy most specific user needs.

Arts	Games	Politics
Business	Health	Recreation
Chat	Internet	Reference
Computers	Kids	Science
Education	Life	Sports
Entertainment	News	Travel

WebCrawler has the best Help pages of any of the search tools we have reviewed. The Help information is well organized into a variety of categories. Individual pages contain useful examples and clear explanations. WebCrawler even goes so far as to include simple diagrams of its primary functions and component parts (such as its databases and robots).

RESULTS AND RANKING

WebCrawler presents the user's search results in ranked order, based on the number of times search words appear in a page. In addition, search words that WebCrawler judges to be less common on the Web as a whole receive higher scores than more common search words. WebCrawler does not describe its ranking process in any further detail.

At the top of each page of results sits a search form containing the user's query. The user may revise his or her search strategy on the form, without returning to the original search page. Below this form WebCrawler reports the total number of hits retrieved in the search. Beneath the total lies a button that allows the user to change the display of the search results; if the original request was for results that include summaries, the user may switch to the one-line title display, and vice versa.

The title display presents the results as hot-linked titles or URLs. If a page has been reviewed by WebCrawler's staff, a small *Review* image follows the title. To the left of each title is a small icon. The degree to which the icon is shaded indicates a rough approximation of the page's rank score. Given that the results are presented in ranked order, this is not very useful information.

Each hit in the summaries display consists of the title of the page, followed by an automatically generated summary, the percentage ranking score, the URL, and a link to a *Similar Pages* search function. WebCrawler generates its summaries from the initial text of Web pages during the harvesting/indexing process. If the page begins with information other than text, such as Java script or other coded instructions, the summary will appear as gibberish to the user.

Warren Zevon Home Page!

The scope of this has changed. scope creep scope creep I am going to make this a cute little Warren Zevon Trivia Challenge, using forms and either cgi or java to have a real quiz form, which will be graded on line. I'm also going to restructure the albums ...
- Score 95% - *http://sushi.st.usm.edu/%7Ehamorris/zevon.html* - *Find Similar Pages*

If the user finds a particularly interesting or relevant page in the results, he or she may instruct WebCrawler to perform an automatic search that attempts to find pages "similar" to the relevant one. WebCrawler creates this search by identifying keywords in the original document (defined by their frequency of occurrence in the body of the page) and connecting them with Boolean **OR**. Most of the search tools we have reviewed offer a similar function. Our experience has been that this option is generally no better than surfing, especially in WebCrawler's case. We recommend that users begin surfing from the links in the relevant document, rather than ask WebCrawler to look for pages it judges to be similar.

SUMMARY

WebCrawler has the simplest and most user-friendly interface of all of the search tools we review. Its Help documentation is by far the best, both in depth and clarity of information about itself and robot-based search tools in general. Its index is smaller than those of the other tools (so a search may produce only 100,000 hits, rather than 1,000,000), but more problematic is the fact that it is slower to discover new and updated documents.

*Pictures reproduced with the permission of Excite, Inc.

Chapter 7

Lycos

http://www.lycos.com

HISTORY

Lycos was developed by a team at Carnegie Mellon University's Center for Machine Translation. Lycos officially went online for public use on August 12, 1994. The name Lycos was derived from the Latin word *Lycosidae*, a family of ground spiders that actively hunt prey at night rather than using a web. Lycos's developers felt this was an accurate description of their spider, which hunts URLs at night.

Carnegie Mellon formed a number of partnerships with information providers to license the Lycos indexing and searching software. Microsoft's licensing of Lycos for use on the Microsoft Network (MSN) in April 1995 is a typical example. Through this agreement, Microsoft gained use of Lycos, while Carnegie Mellon retained ownership of Lycos and provided updates to Microsoft. NlightN, Inmagic, and others have since licensed Lycos as well.

CMG@Ventures formed an exclusive partnership with Lycos in June 1995. In this case, CMG@Ventures paid a fee to Carnegie Mellon for Lycos and formed a new company, Lycos, Inc. Dr. Michael Mauldin, developer of Lycos, received a minority stake in the company. The purpose of the new company is to enhance technical resources while still providing free Web access. Lycos, Inc., provides advertising space and licenses portions of its software in the burgeoning corporate intranet market.

HOW LYCOS ADDS DOCUMENTS TO ITS DATABASE

Determining the setup of the Lycos index proved much more difficult than for any other search tools we tested, partly because Lycos does not index the full text of Web documents. This feature makes it difficult to determine what facet of a document has brought about its retrieval in a user search.

Lycos defines Web space to include all HTTP, Gopher, and FTP documents. Lycos refuses to harvest any URL containing CGI-like characters (such as ? and =), due to conflicts with the meaning of these characters within Lycos's programming language. Lycos claims to be working on this problem. Its harvester robot, Scout, gathers URLs using a depth-first strategy. Scout begins a round of searching with a somewhat random choice among a set of URLs taken from links in pages that Lycos has already harvested. Thus the results of past work determine the robot's next move. Scout examines a Web page and, if it appears worth indexing (that is, if it fits a given set of parameters, which Lycos does not describe), places the URL in a different queue for another robot to harvest and index at a later date. Scout updates the main Lycos list of pages to be harvested once a week.

Once Scout has identified a page as worth indexing, Lycos sends a second robot to collect the page's title, headings and subheadings; its 100 most weighty words (based on an algorithm considering such factors as word placement and frequency); its first 20 lines; its file size in bytes; and its total number of words. Lycos stores all of this information like a library catalog record, with a URL as the call number. Part of the textual information is also integrated into the Lycos retrieval index, linking the catalog record to the search words in the index via the URL. Thus, not all of the text that the user sees on a results page is searched in a user query. A page summary may contain words that Lycos did not consider weighty enough to add to its retrieval index.

The fact that Lycos only indexes the "first 20 lines" of a document is also significant. We had trouble determining exactly what Lycos does index, because Lycos provides no information about what constitutes the first 20 lines of a Web page, Gopher document, or FTP file. It does not seem to mean the first 20 lines of tagged HTML code, nor does it seem to be the first 20 lines of text viewed through the user's browser. In fact, it is the browser that determines the number of lines on a screen, not the HTML code. Frequently, the first 20 lines of a document contain little or no textual information, but instead house links to picture files, Java script, or other code. In cases like these, Lycos may not index anything except the title.

Lycos does not seem to index URLs for user searches at all. We searched for a specific page in its catalog, using terms from the text and the URL. The terms in the text were highlighted in the results, but not the terms in the URL, nor was the page retrievable with terms that occur only in its URL. Since Lycos does not index the URL, the only way to retrieve an unharvested page is to rely on the textual content of neighboring documents on the same server. When the Scout robot decides a page is worth indexing, it puts the URL in a list for future harvesting. Until this harvesting occurs, the URL is linked to the "100 weighty words" that Lycos has already indexed from previous encounters with neighboring pages. In this way the user does get access to all of the almost 60 million URLs Lycos has collected, even when their content has not been indexed. The relevance of the hits, however, depends a great deal on the structure of the Web server—if a server does not gather documents into subject neighborhoods in its file structure, the user just gets more clutter in the results set.

INTERFACE AND SEARCHING

Lycos's initial page consists of a single command line for entering search terms and a series of links to other reference tools (for example a map server and Sites by Subject) discussed below. Banner ads cover the top quarter of the page. It is unfortunate that Lycos and several other search engines fail to include on the initial search screen any brief instruction or examples of how to create a search. Users are usually forced two or three links deep into the Help files to find examples. (In contrast, obvious links transport the user from the search screen to advertising information, advertisers' sites, and detailed instructions for making Lycos one's home page.) Users who skip Lycos's Help miss very little. Lycos seems very pleased with itself for having abandoned the ubiquitous FAQ format for organizing Help information, but it has failed to provide most of the information a FAQ usually contains. Most of the Help documentation dwells on nonsearch features and it offers no examples.

I want to search

LYCOS It's amazing where Go Get It will get you. Lycos' Halloween Hotlist

The Web   for: [   ] Go Get It ▶ Custom Search

Custom Search
Site Map
Inside Lycos
Club Lycos
Free Software
New 2 Net

On Lycos Now:

Screams Across the Web: A special Halloween presentation
Millennium Watch: Prepare for the end
GVU's Web user survey: Become a statistic!

Top News   Sites by Subject
Top 5% Sites   City Guide
Pictures & Sounds   People Find
Point Review   Road Maps

Lycos does offer an "advanced" search option, accessible through the cryptically named *Custom Search* link next to the *Simple* search command line. The *Custom Search* form also offers a single command line, along with five drop-down menus from which users may choose operators, an index to search (either all types of Web pages and files, Web sound or picture files, or Sites by Subject), and restrictions on the number of hits listed and the display form for the search results.

Besides Web searches, users may link to Lycos's two other Web entry points, Point and Sites by Subject (sometimes referred to as a2z). Point offers an index of reviews of Web sites. Point employs reviewers to identify what they judge to be the "top 5%" of the Web, give each such page a numerical rating based on content and presentation, and write a paragraph review. Users may search the index of reviews using the *Simple* Lycos search form or browse a subject hierarchy. The Sites by Subject service provides access to an index of the most popular sites on the Web, defined as those sites that have greater than a given threshold of links to them from other sites on the Web. Users browse down a subject hierarchy to reach specific sites, each of which has a description written by editors at Lycos.

SEARCH OPTIONS AND OPERATORS

Lycos offers little flexibility for creating searches. Users may enter one or more keywords in the command line of either the *Simple* or *Custom* search forms. In both types of searches, Lycos automatically connects multiple terms with Boolean *OR*, retrieving all pages in its index that contain any of the search terms. Users may not type Boolean operators themselves to connect query words. A minus sign (-) preceding a word acts something like the *NOT* operator, but not by excluding pages containing the word from the results set—instead, in the ranking process, it pushes those pages toward the bottom of the ranked list. Users may not search for phrases or for words appearing in a particular order or within a given proximity of one another. Lycos also ignores case and punctuation. Lycos will not search for words composed entirely of numbers (such as the year *1996*), nor words that begin with numbers (such as **3D**), but it will retrieve words *containing* numbers after the initial character (such as **R2D2**).

In addition to the minus sign, users have two other symbols at their disposal. A period (.) at the end of a search term will force Lycos to search only for the word as the user has typed it—no plural forms or alternate endings will be retrieved. On the other hand, the dollar sign ($) at the end of a word serves as a truncation symbol, telling Lycos to search for any word beginning with the character string the user has typed.

One may ask, "Why does Lycos need both the period and dollar sign operators?" Good question—it would seem that Lycos would either default to a search of the words as they are typed or default to a truncation process to search more broadly. If so, the user would need only one of the operators to carry out the non-default alternative.

In fact, Lycos does perform a default truncation on user search words, as long as the words are composed of more than three characters. When the user enters a term, Lycos automatically searches for other words that begin with the characters the user entered. For example, from the user search

Netscape - [Welcome to Lycos]

File   Edit   View   Go   Bookmarks   Options   Directory   Window   Help

[Back] [Forward] [Home]   [Reload] [Images] [Open] [Print] [Find]   [Stop]

Location: http://www.lycos.com/

[What's New!] [What's Cool!] [Handbook]   [Net Search] [Net Directory] [Software]

[Top 5% Sites] [CityGuide] [Pictures&Sounds] [PeopleFind] [StockFind] [RoadMaps]

LYCOS
Your
Personal
Internet Guide

Search [The Web ▼] for: [frog]   [Go Get It]

CUSTOM SEARCH

UNISYS   Click here

Need Help?
Start Here.

YELLOW PAGES
COMPANIES ONLINE
UPS™ SERVICES
CLASSIFIEDS
LYCOS PRESS
FREE SOFTWARE
LINK TO LYCOS
INSIDE LYCOS

NEWS	SPORTS	MONEY
TRAVEL	TECHNOLOGY	HEALTH
SCIENCE	EDUCATION	LIFESTYLE
CULTURE	SHOPPING	KIDS
BUSINESS	ENTERTAINMENT	CAREERS
FASHION	GOVERNMENT	AUTOS

ON LYCOS NOW
• Hot New Lycos Look!
• April Fools?
• Explore the Isles
• O Canada..
• Online Tax Guide

Get Lycos or get lost

Lycos Germany ▪ Lycos Sweden ▪ Lycos France

Document: Done

Lycos will retrieve both **frog** and **frogs**. But if the user follows the word with a period, Lycos will retrieve only **frog**. We have never detected any difference between the default truncation process and the use of the dollar sign. Apparently the dollar sign is vestigial.

Neither truncation approach will retrieve every word beginning with the user term, however. It seems as though Lycos only looks for certain variations, such as simple plurals and some verb endings. The previous example retrieves both **frog** and **frogs**, but not **froggy** or **frogmen**. Lycos may refer to a handpicked list of word variations to find multiple word forms, but it probably uses a list of common word suffixes and generic rules for applying them to any word.

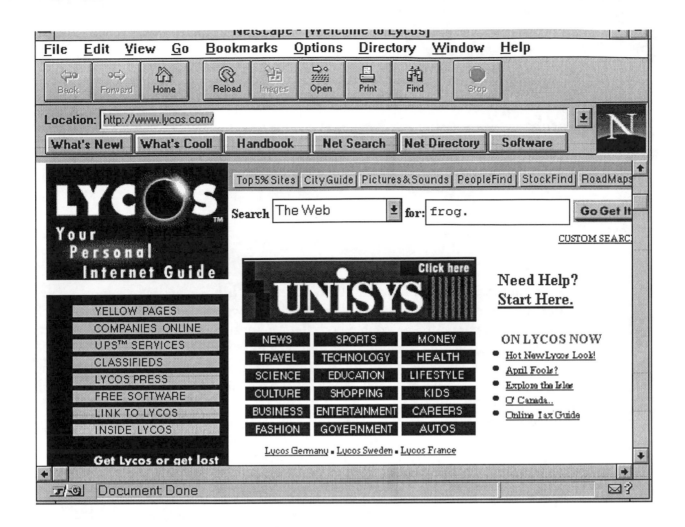

With Lycos's *Custom* search form, the user has several more options. The single command line remains from the *Simple* search, but one of the pull-down menus contains approximations of the **OR** and **AND** operators. As we mentioned, Lycos connects multiple terms with **OR** by default in both *Simple* and *Custom* searches. In addition to this option, the menu allows the user to connect all of the terms in the command line with **AND**. Further, users can limit the search to pages containing any two to seven of the search terms. These latter options are most useful for searching with alternate spellings.

For example, if the user were to limit the search to pages containing any two of the following three terms

Customize Your Search

Search: | The Web ▲▼ | **for:** | labor labour movemen |

Search Options: | match 2 terms ▲▼ |

| loose match ▲▼ |

each page will contain *labor* and *movement*, or *labour* and *movement*, or *labor* and *labour,* or all three. Although the latter two cases are unlikely, the search will cover documents mentioning both the American and British labor movements (or labor movements in general written by authors in either country). However, if the user had connected all three terms with the blanket *AND* menu option, the search would have retrieved only pages containing both spellings—a much smaller set.

Lycos does maintain a list of stopwords, and those words are ignored in a user query. While Lycos does not provide the list to the user, stopwords are not displayed in the list (at the top of the results page) of words it did search. The presence of stopwords in a query does not cause the search to fail. Lycos does not specify how it derives its list of stopwords.

RESULTS AND RANKING

Lycos is at its best and its worst when presenting search results. First the good points. As we mentioned above, unless the user adds a period after a search word, Lycos will automatically truncate the word to search for some variant endings. When this happens, Lycos lists some of the terms it searched for at the top of the page of results. Each such term then becomes a hotlink. For example, if the user searched for the word *germ*, the top of the results page might appear

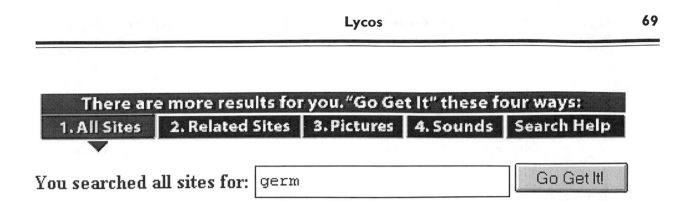

If the user clicks on the word/link **_german_**, Lycos will perform a search for that word alone, as if it were followed by a period. Not only do users get to see the relative frequency of various forms of their search terms in the Lycos index, but they may perform a very easy search on each of the forms. If the user initially searches for multiple terms, each of those terms and some of their derivatives will appear as hotlinks in the results. Lycos gets a gold star for this feature.

Unfortunately, the results of this function are not consistent, rendering the truncation process unpredictable. We could never determine how Lycos decides which terms to search with the truncation process. Recall that **germ** retrieved **german**, **germany**, and presumably other variations indicated by the ellipsis. Some terms retrieve more (and others less) than three variations; some receive ellipses, others do not. Further, unknown variations often represent a large portion of the results—the search statement **germ** pulled almost 50,000 hits, but the words **germ, german**, and **germany** accounted for fewer than 20,000 of those. The unknown variations on the initial search term accounted for more than half of the hits retrieved.

Each hit in the results page is composed of a hotlinked title, a summary generated automatically from the first 200 characters of the Web page, the page's URL and file size, and a ranking score. Lycos does not recognize HTML meta tags for keywords or author summaries. As a result, many page summaries are just gibberish, generated from Java script or other nontextual matter present at the beginning of the page.

Lycos does print user search terms in bold type where they appear in the summaries, which is helpful. In addition, at the bottom of a results page Lycos offers an *Edit Your Search* form. The form offers a command line containing the current search terms (for editing) and check-boxes for choosing to *Match All Words* (that is, connect them with Boolean **AND**) or *Match Any Word* (that is, connect them with Boolean **OR**).

Previous Page   Next Page
Jump down the list:
Previous 10 Pages   Next 10 Pages

Edit your search: [   ]

[Go Get It!]

○ Match all words ● Match any word

Users searching from the *Custom* form may choose from two other display options in a pull-down menu. The *Summary* option displays the results just as a hotlinked title and a ranking score. The *Standard* option offers the title, ranking, size, a line from the page containing a user search term or an abstract, and the URL. The *Detailed* option contains (if the information is available) the title, ranking, number of outside links, matched words, outline, abstract, description, URL, file size, and date updated.

Unique to the *Custom* form are the *Type of Match* and *Number of Results* options. With the *Number of Results* option, the user may choose to receive search hits in groups of 20, 30, or 40 at a time, rather than the default 10. The *Type of Match* option will restrict the results of a search to only those items scoring above a given percentage in Lycos's ranking process. Users may choose among *Loose, Fair, Good, Close,* and *Strong. Loose* is the default, returning everything matching the search, no matter the score. *Fair* returns items with *30 percent* relevancy or better; *Good, Close,* and *Strong* return items with 50 percent, 70 percent, and 90 percent relevancy or better, respectively.

Lycos presents its results in ranked order. Pages whose titles contain terms from the user's search receive higher scores, as do those with multiple search terms, especially when the terms are in close proximity to one another. The score is calculated from the information stored in the Lycos catalog about the page. Since Lycos only retains a small portion of each document it indexes, proximity of search terms is unlikely to be a significant factor. Multiple search terms will generally be proximal in small portions of documents.

A significant problem with Lycos's search results is the number of redundant URLs. The *Custom* search

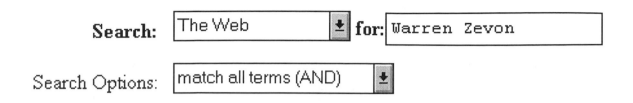

using the *Match All Terms* option, retrieved 29 URLs. Of these, seven were duplicates. The search

connected by the *Match All Terms* option retrieved 50 close URLs. Sixteen of these were duplicate URLs. Since users also often retrieve the same document from different sites with different URLs, Lycos's redundancy can be a nuisance.

On the other end of the results spectrum, if the user's search retrieves nothing, Lycos responds with a brief Help message, which recommends that the user try searching for a shorter stem of the original term. For example, if **frogs** got you nowhere, try **frog**. The message also informs the user that Lycos found no words beginning with the failed term, but this is unhelpful and sometimes untrue. Since Lycos truncates by default, the presence of words beginning with the failed search term would produce some hits and no failure message at all, unless the original search was restricted by the user. A search for **netonl** retrieved 62 hits, but due only to the variant forms *netonline* and *netonly*.

Top 5% Sites | CityGuide | Pictures&Sounds | PeopleFind | StockFind | RoadMaps

Search [The Web ▼] for: [netonl.   ] [Go Get It]

CUSTOM SEARCH

Searching for *netonl* with a period following it retrieved nothing, followed by the contradictory message that Lycos found no words beginning with *netonl*.

SUMMARY

Lycos's interface is weak and sometimes confusing, offering little flexibility for constructing searches. It provides insufficient information about its searching, indexing, or retrieval processes, leaving users to wonder why they retrieve the results they do. Since it only indexes parts of documents, its overall retrieval suffers in comparison to many other search tools. Lycos's best features are in its presentation of search results. Overall, Lycos does not measure up to most of its competitors.

Chapter 8

Infoseek

http://www.infoseek.com

HISTORY

Infoseek Corporation was founded in January 1994 by Steven Kirsch. It went public in June 1996, trading on NASDAQ as SEEK. Infoseek supports itself through third-party advertising. Infoseek introduced the first CPM (cost per thousand impressions) model of advertising to the Internet. CPM establishes a base unit for selling ads—Infoseek charges a set price for the assurance that a company's ad will be accessed 1,000 times by Internet users. For example, assume Infoseek's rate is $1 for 1,000 viewings. If a user (or a mix of users) performed 1,000 Infoseek searches, and an ad for Kentucky Fried Chicken (KFC) appeared at the top of each results set, KFC owes Infoseek $1. If the ad were viewed a million times, then KFC would owe $1,000. This pricing model attempts to transfer the established readership-based pricing model for ad rates from the print publications industry. Magazines figure their ad rates based on the number of subscribers or the average number of copies each issue sells, since this gives an idea of how many people will see the ads. This is roughly analogous to the number of viewings, or "impressions," of a Web banner ad.

We want to note that Infoseek is the exception to the rule that Web search tools do not change substantively over time. Search tools continually add and remove features like map and news servers, subject directories, and other tools to improve access. Infoseek has done this as well, but it has also substantially rebuilt its index and revised its user search capabilities. It is worth noting that Infoseek's newest incarnation required several months of index building and beta testing as a separate tool called *Infoseek Ultra* (plus two years in planning and development, as Infoseek frequently points out), illustrating that it is not easy for these tools to truly reform.

HOW INFOSEEK ADDS DOCUMENTS TO ITS DATABASE

Infoseek's robot harvests daily, collecting Usenet postings and Web pages. Infoseek claims to revisit and reharvest each of the pages in its Web index over the course of three to four weeks. We routinely retrieved pages whose URLs indicated that they lie deep within the file structures of their home Web sites, suggesting that Infoseek's robot may be harvesting more deeply than its competitors.

Infoseek harvests the full text of the Web pages it discovers. Its index appears to be very extensive and relatively current. To up the ante on speed, Infoseek offers "real-time" indexing of URLs submitted by users. We tested this and found that if a user submits the URL of a new Web page, Infoseek usually adds the URL to its index within minutes. But this is *only* the URL—we could not determine how long it takes for Infoseek to harvest the text of a newly submitted URL.

Infoseek also claims to be able to keep track of how often individual Web pages change, so that it can update their indexing on a frequency-of-change schedule. But our searches for some rapidly changing pages found weeks-old entries and months-old summaries. We only found one or two dead links in our search results, so Infoseek seems to be doing a good job of getting rid of old and missing links—but we tested its new index so early that it probably had not been around long enough to accumulate many.

Infoseek does recognize author-attached HTML meta tags designating keywords and author-provided summaries. When Infoseek harvests a Web page with a meta tag labeled *description*, it uses the content as the summary of the page in user search results, rather than automatically generating a summary from the first 200 characters of the page's body. The author is limited, however, to 200 characters for the summary. Infoseek indexes the content of keyword meta tags as it would any other text in the page, with no additional weighting or marking. Authors may include up to 1,000 characters worth of keywords in the meta tag, but if a single keyword is repeated more than seven times (a common author tactic for getting a page to rank high in search results) Infoseek will ignore the field.

INTERFACE AND SEARCHING

Infoseek maintains two different search interfaces. The first, *Ultrasmart*, offers a standard command line, a pull-down menu of searchable databases, a Yahoo!-style list of browsable subject headings, and links to secondary sources (such as cartographic and e-mail databases). Infoseek does not produce these secondary databases, but links to them on their respective home servers. The Web searching portion of the interface is presently one of the simplest available. It consists of a single command line for typing keywords or natural language queries, followed by one drop-down menu for choosing an index to search. Users can choose between *the Web, Usenet Newsgroups, News Wires, Premier News, E-mail Addresses, Company Profiles*, and *Web FAQs*. Ultrasmart offers Help through its *Tips* link next to the command line.

The Ultraseek interface is basically the same as Ultrasmart, only without the browsable classification system below the command line. Infoseek claims that Ultraseek is for the more advanced searcher who wants to use the special features of Infoseek's search engine, but every feature in Ultraseek is equally available in Ultrasmart. The *Tips* link under the command line takes the user to the same Help files as Ultrasmart.

Infoseek has definitely improved its Help documentation since its early incarnations, although it is still incomplete. The Tips are organized under headings (which are slow to browse fully); they are informative, although they sound like an ad for a used car. Infoseek also tends to clutter its Help files with inappropriate and questionable comparisons between itself and other Web search tools, although it is not alone in this practice. Excessive cheerleading is just one more unfortunate incentive for users to ignore Help.

Infoseek uses Xerox Linguistic Technology (XLT) in its search engine to manipulate keywords and phrases in user queries. When searching, XLT automatically maps user keywords to their lexical variants (such as plurals and verb conjugates) and user phrases to partial matches. Users can circumvent this feature by enclosing phrases and keywords in quotation marks, forcing exact matches. XLT does much of the work of truncation and wildcard operators, but it does not cover everything. For example, the search

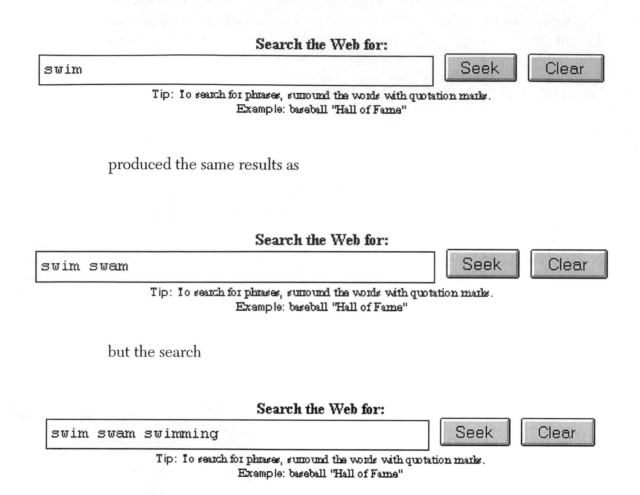

produced the same results as

but the search

produced over 50,000 more hits than the previous two. These and other examples suggest that XLT misses common endings for some words. Unfortunately, Infoseek does not offer the user a truncation or wildcard operator to pick up the slack.

Users can indicate phrases in a search statement by enclosing them in quotation marks, connecting each word with a hyphen, or capitalizing the first letter of one or more of the keywords. Infoseek is case sensitive—user keywords or phrases containing any capitalized letters will force exact matches, while keywords typed all in lower case retrieve any case. Infoseek interprets two adjacent capitalized words as a proper name and searches them as a phrase. This name searching feature only spares users the effort of putting the name in quotation marks—it retrieves neither inverted names, nor names with middle initials (for example, **John Smith** would retrieve neither **Smith, John** nor **John A. Smith**).

In fact, users should understand that Infoseek may interpret pairs of unrelated keywords as names. This happened to us on occasion. For example, the search

No Results Found

You searched for...
Tyberious' Mother

[   ] seek

returned no results, since the capitalization caused Infoseek to treat the statement as an actual name. The search

infoseek®

You searched for **tyberious' mother**

Sites 1 - 10 of 465,900

retrieved several thousand hundred hits. Users must separate multiple phrases
and names in the same search with commas.

Infoseek eschews Boolean operators in favor of plus (+) and minus (-) signs.
Infoseek joins multiple search terms with Boolean **OR** by default (unless they
are capitalized, as mentioned earlier). The ranking process pushes those results
matching all the search terms to the top of the list. The user may approximate
Boolean **AND** by inserting a plus sign in front of each word that he or she wants
to appear in every page of the results. Hence the query

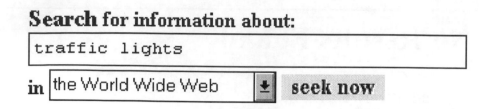

may produce many pages about drug trafficking and Christmas lights, in addition to those about traffic lights. In order to ensure that traffic lights are the focus, a better search is

Infoseek ignores the plus and minus signs when they appear in front of common words, such as **computer**. It does not elaborate on how common a word must be to trigger this response.

Users may place plus and minus sign operators in front of phrases, in the same manner as with keywords. All of the following are syntactically correct Infoseek searches that retrieve pages with **peace,** but do not contain specific forms of the phrase **Nobel Prize**:

Type a **specific question, "phrase in quotes"** or **Capitalized Name**.

```
peace -Nobel Prize
```

the Web   ↕   seek   **Tips**

Type a **specific question, "phrase in quotes"** or **Capitalized Name**.

```
peace -"nobel prize"
```

the Web   ↕   seek   **Tips**

Type a **specific question, "phrase in quotes"** or **Capitalized Name**.

```
peace -nobel -prize
```

| the Web | ± | seek | **Tips**

Infoseek's *pipe* (|) operator is an interesting approximation of Boolean **AND**. Typing a keyword, followed by a space, the pipe (|) symbol, and then a second keyword forces Infoseek to retrieve all pages containing the first keyword, and then to search this resulting set for pages that contain the second keyword. For example,

Type a **specific question, "phrase in quotes"** or **Capitalized Name**.

```
government |president
```

| the Web | ± | seek | **Tips**

would send Infoseek to find all pages in its index that contain the word *government*, and then look at the results and find all of the *government* pages that contain the word *president*. Users can do the same thing by searching for *government* alone in the Ultrasmart command line, then searching for *president* in the command line at the bottom of the *government* results page (as long as the "Search only these results" option below the command line is checked).

Click here for more information

You searched for **government**

```
president
```
| seek | **Tips**

⦿ Search **only** these results   ◯ Search **the whole Web**

Remember... Wear your seatbelts.

Many readers may be asking themselves, "But isn't this *pipe* operator the same thing as Boolean **AND** (or in Infoseek's case, two plus signs)? Wouldn't **+government +president** retrieve the same results? And, by the way, where is the *pipe* key on my keyboard? " Logically, the pipe operator and Boolean **AND** are identical, since both retrieve all of the documents containing both keywords, and only those documents. In fact, the pipe and (+) searches do retrieve the same documents from Infoseek—the difference between the two sets of results lies in the order in which the documents are ranked. Why are they ranked differently? Probably because Infoseek is performing the same steps in both searches, but in a different order, or because it adds or removes a step or two, or a combination of both. Further illustrating this difference, the search statements **+government +president** and **+president +government** retrieve identical results (both in content and rank order), while the searches **government |president** and **president |government** retrieve the same documents as the former two, but each with a different ranking order from the other *three*. To put it another way, these four search statements all retrieve the same documents, but provide a choice of three ranking orders for the results. The only problem here is that, since Infoseek neglects to describe its ranking process in any depth, the user is left with no way to decide *which* of these three choices would be better in any given situation. We have experimented with each, but could find no consistent reason, short of which was quicker to type, to prefer one formula over another,. Surprisingly, for two out of three of us, typing the two plus signs was quicker than the single pipe sign, since we kept forgetting where the pipe sign is on our keyboards (it's on the same key as the backslash—common knowledge of the computer programming intelligentsia, especially at Infoseek, but little known by many users).

Infoseek also lets users restrict keyword or phrase searches to four HTML fields. A *Link* search searches the URLs of links within the body of a Web page, as opposed to a *URL* search, which retrieves pages whose URLs contain the word. Thus the search

Enter a URL in the form below. Infoseek Ultra will count and list the pages that match this URL. Do not put any blank spaces in the form.

```
url:david.com
```
[Seek] [Reset]

url:netscape will show you the pages Infoseek Ultra has in its index that have netscape in their URLs.

would retrieve the page whose URL is ***http://david.com***, while the search

Enter a URL in the form below, and Infoseek Ultra will count and list the pages that have links to it. Do not put any blank spaces in the form.

```
link:david.com
```
[Seek] [Reset]

link:infoseek.com will find pages that link to Infoseek.

would only retrieve that page if it contained a link to a *different* page with *david.com* in *its* URL. A *Site* search retrieves any pages from a given site, identified by the first portion of the URL. Thus the search

Enter a web site in the form below. Infoseek Ultra will count and list the pages from that site that it has in its index. Do not put any blank spaces in the form.

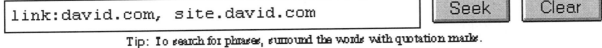

`site:david.com`   Seek   Reset

site:travelocity.com will find all the pages from Travelocity that Infoseek Ultra has in its index.

would retrieve all of the pages Infoseek has harvested from the server named *david.com*, as well as from servers such as *www.david.com* and *super.david.com*. A *Title* search restricts the search to the contents of the HTML <TITLE> field. Field searches must use colons and no spaces, like the examples above. Multiple field searches must be separated with commas, like

Search the Web for:

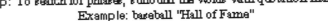

`link:david.com, site.david.com`   Seek   Clear

Tip: To search for phrases, surround the words with quotation marks.
Example: baseball "Hall of Fame"

Infoseek makes a big deal out of its ability to recognize natural language queries. This talent stems primarily from the XLT search engine software and Infoseek's results-ranking algorithms. Since Infoseek does not recognize words like **AND** as operators and omits no stopwords from its index, users need not worry about such words fouling up a search. When the search engine encounters such words in a natural language query, it **OR**s all of the words together, searches for each, then places hits retrieved with traditional stopwords at the bottom of the list. So it does not matter if the user asks, *How should I go to Brooklyn* or *Why should I go to Brooklyn*, because only *Brooklyn* will factor meaningfully into the ranking process. Infoseek focuses on the subject keywords it extracts from the query statement.

Ironically, since this natural language understanding does not actually operate on words like **AND**, queries such as *Get me pages on horses but not flies* and *Get me pages on horses and flies* will retrieve basically the same results. From the user's perspective, Infoseek leaves some of the most critical words in these sentences out of the ranking process. Overall Infoseek seems to handle natural language queries as well as or better than the other search tools that offer the option, but none of these tools can make much out of a complicated natural language statement, especially one with multiple clauses.

RESULTS AND RANKING

Infoseek's search results report the overall number of hits retrieved. However, as with some other search tools, we found it impossible to view hits far down the list. For example, one of our searches retrieved over 13,000 hits, but our attempts to view any hits beyond number 600 returned only banner ads. This significantly devalues the hit totals, from the user's perspective, even though few users would ever venture that far down a list of results (we hope).

Infoseek's results sets often number in the millions. Fortunately, its ranking algorithms work well most of the time (although as we mentioned in the pipe operator discussion, the user cannot exploit this very effectively). Good keyword searches (such as those with three or more terms) and simple natural language queries usually present a desirable page in the top five hits. Infoseek ranks pages based on where query terms occur in the pages (terms near the beginning and in titles rank high), the number of query terms in the page (both the percentage of the query words it contains and the overall number of occurrences), and the rarity of the query words on the Web (e.g., *computer* would rank far lower than the rarer *hemophilia* in the same query). Individual phrases almost always appear less frequently than most individual words on the Web, so phrases essentially work the same as rare words. The order of words in the user query also affects the ranking, with the first keywords in the query ranking higher than those that follow (although this does not happen if the user precedes each term with a plus operator).

In addition to presenting results in ranked order, Infoseek assigns each hit a percentage score from 0 to 100. Many other search tools rank all of the pages in the results set just against each other. This means the first page (relative to all the others) in every set of results will always receive the same maximum score, (such as 100, 1000, or 99%), while the last page will get 0 or 1%. All of the intervening pages receive scores depending on how they compare to the best and worst. Since these numbers only reflect the order in which the results are presented, they do not provide the user with any additional information. In contrast, the best-ranked page in Infoseek's results sets can receive any score from 0 to 100, not just 100. In other words, Infoseek may admit that the best page it could find (that is, the first hit in the results page) is not 100 percent likely to be relevant to the user's need.

Since each set of search results in Infoseek can start off with any score from 0 to 100, there seems to be some sort of objective standard against which Infoseek measures all search results. For example, if the user's first search produces a set whose initial item has a score of 43, but a second search has an initial hit with a score of 57, the implication is that some comparative value exists between the two searches. Each results set is ranked internally to push likely hits to the top of each list, but the different scores between the best hits of each list indicate some sort of comparison between the searches. This is confusing. One interpretation is that Infoseek is providing the user with feedback for improving his or her searches—for example, a search whose first hit has a low score should be revised to include more esoteric terms. But this implies that Infoseek maintains a list ranking all of the words in its Web index by frequency, which it consults when scoring each search it receives. It also implies a belief that infrequent terms are intrinsically better for user searches, which is obviously not always the case (several common terms connected with Boolean **AND** often work better). So far as we can tell, the user may as well ignore numerical scores in Infoseek's search results, for lack of anything better to do with them.

Each hit in the results page consists of a link to a Web page, its URL, its score, the size of the file, and a summary of the contents. Infoseek generates summaries of Web pages automatically from the first 200 characters of text during the indexing process, except when the page's author includes a summary marked with a <META> tag. Automatic summaries usually consist of the HTML <TITLE> and the first few lines of text.

Infoseek provides a command line at the bottom of each page of the search results, for users to revise their searches. One detail of this command line marks one of two (barely) significant differences between the Ultrasmart and Ultraseek interfaces. In the results of an Ultrasmart search, the revision command line does not arrive with the previous search statement already filled in; instead, it provides a check-box for restricting the revised search to the set of current search results or for sending it to search the entire index again. In the results of an Ultraseek search, the revision command line arrives with the previous search statement already filled in, but without a check-box to restrict the revised search to the current set of search results—thus Infoseek automatically searches the entire index again. The second difference between the two interfaces lies at the top of the results page, where Ultrasmart reports only the number of hits in the results set, but where Ultraseek also includes the number of hits it found for each word or phrase in the query.

SUMMARY

Infoseek seems to be a fast and thorough indexer. It ranks results relatively well, and it processes natural language queries as well as or better than any other Web search tool. It also links itself with quite a few useful specialized tools, although any user tempted to try Infoseek's browsable subject headings should instead just go to Yahoo! (Infoseek brags that its browsing index is the largest available, but such tools are only valuable if they are well organized, especially when they are large—for example, Bill Gates has his own subject heading, but it is under *Entertainment, Celebrities, Bill Gates.*) Infoseek does not need two nearly identical interfaces (the only reason to use the "streamlined" Ultraseek, instead of Ultrasmart, is to avoid looking at a few classification headings), especially when both are weak and cryptic. Infoseek clutters its site with the most self-promotion (especially inflated claims and comparisons) of any search engine we have used. Searchers who want to perform lengthy or complicated queries (especially queries requiring Boolean operators) could do much better with other tools, such as AltaVista and HotBot, which have more flexibility and features. Given that Infoseek's best feature is its speed and depth of indexing the Web, we usually employ it as a secondary tool, to supplement searches from other engines with better interfaces.

---

*Pictures reprinted by permission. Infoseek, Ultrasmart, Ultraseek, iSeek, Quickseek, ImageSeek, Ultrashop, "proof of intelligent life on the net" and the Infoseek logos are trademarks of Infoseek Corporation which may be registered in certain jurisdictions. Other trademarks shown are trademarks of their respective owners.

Chapter 9

Open Text

http://index.opentext.net

HISTORY

Like several other Web search tools we evaluate, Open Text exists to advertise the power of its searching and indexing software. Now publicly owned (OTEXF on NASDAQ), the Open Text corporation has existed in some form since around 1990. It is a Canadian company founded on technology developed by Tim Bray at the University of Waterloo in the late 1980s. Open Text merged with Odesta Corporation in 1995 to develop a set of intranet products that allow corporate customers to develop their own systems of document management, local searching, workflow, and Internet use.

HOW OPEN TEXT ADDS DOCUMENTS TO ITS DATABASE

Open Text's index lacks depth. Open Text's Livelink Spider crawls the Internet daily to add and update links to the index. Open Text claims to add approximately 50,000 pages per day to its index. The company says that the Livelink Spider can be configured to index a server in depth, but they do not seem to do this for their demonstration Web index, which limits what a user can retrieve. For example, the musical group Rainmakers has a home page at http://www.sky.net/~hoss/rain.html. The page has been available since the beginning of 1996. Open Text contains over 1,200 pages that reside on or are linked to the www.sky.net server, but that home page cannot be retrieved from Open Text as of September 1996. No search tool can index everything, but Open Text does brazenly claim to search "Every Word, Every Page, Everywhere."[1]

The Livelink Spider and the indexing software are part of Open Text's package of intranet products. As is usually the case with vendors, detailed information about the software's composition and behavior is not available. The Livelink Spider harvests by following links from Web pages it has already visited. Open Text claims that it recognizes the structure of documents on the Web (or in your office, as the case may be), and that the index treats them accordingly. Those who purchase the intranet system can customize the spider to index more often and more intensively, but the freely available Open Text Web index does not seem to take advantage of these more advanced features. The index does not interpret HTML Meta tags or other optional HTML subject tags. The index does not preserve case, nor does it identify or omit any controlled set of stopwords. Open Text indexes Usenet in addition to the Web.

Open Text uses 14 64-bit servers "working in tandem" to create and store its index. These servers receive a user query and process it in parallel across the entire index on the 14 servers. While working on this chapter during the spring/summer of 1996, we found a problem with inconsistent results, especially in late May and June. We performed the same searches and received different results several times. The most likely explanation is that our requests were routed to different servers. The servers were using varying copies of the index, updated on different schedules, and thus producing different results for the same search request. Since September 1996 (through this writing, in early 1997), the problem seems to have been fixed.

INTERFACE AND SEARCHING

The original Open Text interface offered three different search options: *Simple*, *Compound* (or *Power*) and *Weighted* searching. Open Text has since redesigned its interface, now only offering *Simple* and *Power* searches. (During the time we were researching this chapter, about three months, Open Text significantly redesigned its interface three times.) Although it remains one of the more flexible and useful interfaces available, the loss of weighted searching is a negative quality. Users must construct searches using menus to choose operators, rather than typing Boolean ***AND***, ***OR***, or ***NOT***.

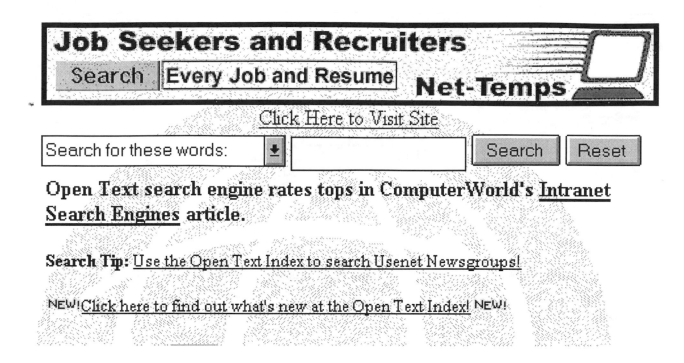

The user is first presented with three options: *Simple* search, *Power* search, or *Japanese Index*. The initial screen's default puts the user into the *Simple* search mode. The *Simple* search mode offers a single command line for creating a simple keyword or phrase query. A drop-down menu in front of the command line allows the user to indicate whether a multiple word search statement should be searched as an exact phrase or as separate keywords. If the user chooses the keyword option, Open Text automatically connects the keywords in the command line with Boolean **AND**. This will return only documents containing both words. One consequence of this feature is that the user cannot perform a search that approximates Boolean **OR**. Given that **OR** searches generally produce tremendous numbers of hits, this is not often a great loss. (In contrast, several other Web search tools allow **OR** searches, but rank resulting pages containing all of the terms ahead of those with only one of the terms—thus the user gets the default **AND** search results first, but can still scan down to the lower-ranked hits that would only result from the **OR** search.) Although the user can create an **OR** search in Open Text's *Power* search mode, the omission of a common function from the default search screen (the *Simple* mode) is worth noting.

The *Power* search option offers a more complicated search interface. The user can perform a keyword or phrase search, similar to the *Simple* search above, but may restrict the search to several areas of the HTML document: *Anywhere*, *Title*, *Summary*, *First Heading*, or *URL*. The default, *Anywhere*, as its name implies, imposes no restriction. Open Text will look for the search statement anywhere in the text of a Web document. *Title* limits the search to the contents of the HTML <TITLE> field assigned by the page's author. *Summary* restricts the search to the summaries that Open Text automatically generates from each page it indexes. Similar to *Title*, *First Heading* restricts the search to the first HTML <HEADING> assigned by the page's author. *URL* limits the search to the URLs of pages in the Open Text index.

A very important point to remember is that Open Text treats query words in the command lines of a *Power* search differently from those in the *Simple* search. Notice that in the *Power* search, there is no menu in front of the command line(s) with which to choose phrase or keyword searching. Unlike the *Simple* search, Open Text automatically treats multiple words in a single *Power* search command line *as a phrase*. To connect multiple keywords with Boolean **AND**, the user *must* put each keyword in a separate command line and choose **AND** from the menu that links the lines. So, the following two cases are identical:

Simple search

The INTERNET **advertising** NETWORK   **DoubleClick**

Click Here to Visit Site

Search for these words: | cat dog | Search | Reset

IDC Rates Open Text Livelink #1 Leader in Intranet Document Management.

New: Take a break-Check out our new Cartoons page!

NEW!Click here to find out what's new at the Open Text Index! NEW!

Power search

what's everybody **looking at?**   Check out this hour's top stocks on **StockMaster**

Click Here to Visit Site

Search for | cat | within | anywhere

and | dog | within | anywhere

and | | within | anywhere

More lines   Search | Reset

IDC Rates Open Text Livelink #1 Leader in Intranet Document Management.

Furthermore, the following two searches are identical:

Simple search

Power search

Although each word in a *Power* search must reside in its own box (unless the user is searching for a phrase), the *Power* search offers more Boolean operators from which to choose. Each command line after the first is preceded by a drop-down menu containing ***AND***, ***OR***, ***BUT***, ***NOT***, ***NEAR***, and ***FOLLOWED BY***. The first three operators connect the boxes above and to the right in the typical Boolean manner. ***NEAR*** searches for pages with the words in the two boxes appearing within 80 characters of each other, in any order. ***FOLLOWED BY*** looks for the words within 80 characters of each other, but they must appear in the same order as in the query (that is, the contents of box 1 before the contents of box 2). Thus a ***NEAR*** search will retrieve all of the same pages as a ***FOLLOWED BY*** search, plus others. We have found that the "80 characters" claim for both of these operators is frequently incorrect. In fact, some proximity searches retrieved pages in which the words were separated by more than 100 *words*!

Open Text indexes every word of every page. It does not have absolute stopwords, but some words cannot be searched as keywords, even though they are searchable as part of a phrase. Users searching for commonly occurring words such as ***is***, ***are***, ***new***, or ***WWW,*** will get a message saying, "Sorry, your search string was empty." Open Text does not explain this error message, but does say that searches for common words put too much strain on its resources, initiating a message saying that too many pages were retrieved. We did not get this particular message, but we assume the situation is the same. There does not seem to be a pattern (other than differences in frequency on the Web) to the words that will not return sets. ***Is*** produces the error message, but ***been*** returns a set. Searching for ***computer*** returns a set, but ***WWW*** does not. The user can, however, perform searches of such common words as part of a phrase, such as ***The Who*** or ***I Know Why the Caged Bird Sings***. Apparently the index is aware of the words in the document and their position, but cannot search for some specific words alone.

The ultimate cause of these problems with common words is probably similar to AltaVista's big weakness: the ranking process. Given that any of these engines is capable of performing a search with results in the millions, in fractions of a second, it seems unlikely that they fall apart even on searches that tap every page in their indexes (none of the search tools claims to hold more than 70 million documents). The ranking process, however, forces the site to compare each of the pages in a set of results with each other. This process is considerably more complicated than the search. As the set size increases, the speed and power required to perform the ranking actions increases at a dramatically higher rate than simple retrieval. This is why AltaVista will search and retrieve results with any word in an Advanced query, as long as the user does not request that the results be ranked. Ranking huge sets is either aborted or a failure. We assume that Open Text's problem is similar.

Open Text does not perform any automatic stemming of words in its index nor of words in the user's query. As we said, it does index the full text of every page it harvests. Unfortunately, the user is not given any method for truncating terms in the search. Thus, for comprehensive searching, the user must remember to include plural forms, alternate spellings and endings, and various verb forms—at least in *Power* searches. Given that *Simple* searches automatically connect multiple terms with **AND**, the user should refrain from including variant word forms in the *Simple* mode. Since the results would only be pages containing all of the forms simultaneously, most such searches would retrieve nothing. In *Power* searches the user can put each variation in its own box preceded by **OR**. This can become tedious.

Open Text's Help documentation is inadequate and poorly maintained. As we mentioned previously, Open Text frequently rebuilds its search interface and the overall structure of the site, but not all of the old Help documentation is removed or disconnected after each remodeling. This can be annoying, and it can also be disastrous to the user who pays attention to the Help. For example, it is very easy to obtain a Help link after a failed search, explaining that Open Text automatically stems or truncates words in the user's search. This is no longer true—in fact, the user has no way at all to truncate in Open Text at this time; the inaccurate Help reflects a former interface structure that has since been abandoned. There is also no direct link to any generation of Help documents or FAQs from the initial search screens. Open Text only actively offers Help after a search has been performed.

The Japanese Index allows users whose browsers are configured for Japanese to search for pages in that language.

RESULTS AND RANKING

Overall Open Text's harvesting process is not very extensive compared to that of some of its competitors. There are a variety of possible explanations for this, such as a philosophy of generous conduct toward the Web servers containing the documents, an attempt to keep duplicates to a minimum in the index, and software limits. Unfortunately, it often means more work for the user. The best hits in accurate searches of the Open Text index often force the user to follow several links to reach the desired page. The searcher must travel deeper into the Web's link structure than the actual search results to find the answer to a query. For example, a search for **Nobel Prize for Literature** and **1995** resulted in a link to Yahoo!'s Literature Prizes page. From there we linked to the Nobel Prize page and from there to the page for 1995, where we found the answer. This situation occurs frequently with Open Text. It claims to be working on the problem.

Results lists always contain a button linking the user to his or her query statement to refine the search. Each title is a link to a page's home site. The user can choose to see excerpts from each page that contain the words or phrases of the search, rather than a summary. This is a very useful feature, but can be confusing if the search word(s) occurs at the end of a page and is then presented out of context. For our evaluation this feature was a convenient way to force Open Text to prove that our search terms appeared in the resulting documents.

The *Find Similar Pages* option associated with each page in the results uses an algorithm that identifies the most frequently occurring words on that page and automatically searches the index for those words. The HTML structure of the document allows Open Text to weight the terms in the <TITLE> or first <HEADING> in this process. The result is ten pages matching the words in the automatic search.

When we tested this feature the results were mediocre at best. We got different results each time we performed the search for similar pages more than once from the same initial link. We performed the same *Find Similar Pages* search from the same Web link ten times and got back nine different sets of links. None of the 90 links gave us useful information related to our initial search. We tried starting from a Usenet article with **cookies.txt** in the subject line. We received ten Usenet articles back, but only numbers 8 and 9 were about the Netscape file cookies.txt. Starting from the Warren Zevon Home Page, we received ten pages, *none* of which contained the words **Warren Zevon**. They had little if anything to do with the original page. We got everything from an announcement of Project Gutenberg's e-texts to Yahoo!'s listing of Music Studios on the Web, but no home pages of similar artists—which other search engines provided via similar features. There were some music links on the original list, but none to specific artists. From studying the page and the links it appears possible that Open Text weights the text in hyperlinks on the original page heavily for the *Find Similar Pages* feature. Ultimately, the placement and frequency of the phrase **Warren Zevon** in the initial page was measured lower in the ranking algorithm than other less relevant words in the text. The *Find Similar Pages* feature really is only useful for improving a very poor initial user query or for launching forth on a tangential topic discovered serendipitously in the results set.

Open Text automatically generates summaries from documents as it indexes them. Summaries consist of the HTML <TITLE>, first <HEADING>, and "some important text extracted from the document." The important text is what Open Text has left after it discards the HTML coding and "figures out what is important" in the first 100 or so words of a document. Surprisingly, when we looked for the summary text in the beginnings of the pages themselves (by following the results link to the pages' home servers) many of the pages had been changed since the last time the spider had visited them. In fact, duplicates and outdated links are a persistent problem for Open Text. Several times we found three or more outdated links per ten links retrieved in the results set. Given Open Text's flexible Livelink Spider, this can be easily reconfigured, so it may not be a problem in the future.

SUMMARY

Open Text's search interface is one of the better ones available on the Web. It is reasonably flexible in its optimum configuration, but complicated searches are tedious to create. Pull-down menus make field searching simple. Users can quickly narrow their searches from the results screen. Unfortunately, Open Text's database is not extensive enough to take full advantage of these options. The gathering process seems perfunctory and incomplete and the spider does a poor job of keeping links updated.

NOTE

1.   Open Text Products and Services, http://www.opentext.com/otm_prod.html, 23 May 1996.

*Pictures reproduced with the permission of the Open Text Corporation.

Chapter 10

AltaVista

http://www.altavista.digital.com

HISTORY

AltaVista began in mid-1995 as an experiment to test new hardware and software developed by Digital Equipment Corporation (DEC). DEC developers saw the rapidly growing Web as a worthy challenge to the speed and power of its new line of servers and to the text-crunching abilities of its index-building and searching software. They decided to use a very fast spider to harvest documents on the Web and Usenet, turn the results into a full-text index of the Web and Usenet, and provide search software and access to it capable of handling high-volume request traffic with great speed. The prize for achieving this goal would be a successful marketing tool, a living advertisement for several products that potential customers would willingly test-drive on a regular basis.

First open to the public in December 1995, AltaVista's index has grown from 16 million Web pages in December to 31 million as of February 1997. Its robot crawls through three million pages on the Web per day. Its indexing software/ server crunches 1GB of text per hour. AltaVista's six-month anniversary also saw an average of over 12 million search requests from Web users per day. In the summer of 1996 AltaVista replaced Open Text as Yahoo!'s official search engine. (Yahoo! maintains a direct link to a search engine to complement its browsable collection of hand-picked pages with a far more comprehensive collection of pages harvested by robots.) Along with growing critical praise, this endorsement suggests that AltaVista is a huge success; in our humble opinion, it is definitely one of the best Web search tools available. Given that its owners produce both its hardware and software, and its purpose is to make both look enticing, its size and flexibility may prove difficult for other Web indexes to match.

HOW ALTAVISTA ADDS DOCUMENTS TO ITS DATABASE

AltaVista provides no information on the robot spider it uses to harvest documents from the Web and Usenet, except that its name is Scooter, it is "the world's fastest spider," and it obeys the robot exclusion standards. This lack of detail is typical of many search tools, reflecting the fact that the software is also a proprietary product for sale. Robot strategies have become trade secrets.

AltaVista indexes the entire textual content of the pages it gathers, including word positions within the documents. In order to speed retrieval and save space, some search tools only record the number of times a term occurs in a Web page, not the positions of the individual words relative to one another within the document. Unlike these, AltaVista's index holds a compressed form of the entirety of the Web pages it has visited. The benefit is greater potential search flexibility and power. Yet this state of affairs may also prove problematic due to copyright issues, since the index essentially holds a copy of every document it harvests.[1]

This approach results in several benefits. Knowing the position of each word allows AltaVista to restrict searches to particular areas or fields within pages, such as the title and URL. It also can take advantage of HTML <META> tags, allowing Web authors to index their pages and create their own summaries, rather than rely on the automatically generated summaries typical of AltaVista's results sets. Users can also include phrases in queries and search for occurrences of terms within a certain distance of one another in a Web page.

AltaVista does not mention the frequency with which it is updated. It appears to be updated at least monthly.

INTERFACE AND SEARCHING

AltaVista provides separate interface screens for its *Advanced* and *Simple* searches. Upon arrival the user is automatically presented with the *Simple* search screen, although both options are clearly displayed as buttons at the top of the page.

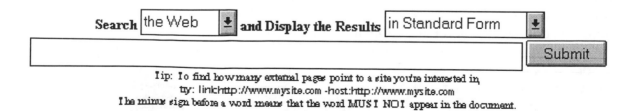

Tip: To find how many external pages point to a site you're interested in, try: link:http://www.mysite.com -host:http://www.mysite.com
The minus sign before a word means that the word MUST NOT appear in the document.

The *Simple* search interface consists of a single command line, similar to that of WebCrawler and others. Above the command line are two pull-down menus. One menu allows the user to switch the search from the Web (the default setting) to Usenet. The other menu defines how the search results will be displayed. In Standard form (the default) each item in the results list contains a multiline summary, either generated automatically by AltaVista from the initial words of the Web page or written by the page's author and marked with a <META> tag to alert AltaVista to use it. The Compact form restricts each displayed hit to a single line, consisting of the title hyperlink, the date AltaVista discovered the page, and a half-line summary. The Detailed form generally looks just like the Standard form. The most glaring omission from the *Simple* search screen is any examples or guides describing how to formulate a query. Given the somewhat arcane syntax involved in these queries, this omission is regrettable. It is offset somewhat by a good Help page, accessible from a button at the top of the screen. The Help contains many clear examples and suggestions, with explanations (unlike other search tools) of why many types of searches fail. Like most search tools, however, it provides little if any discussion of its own shortcomings.

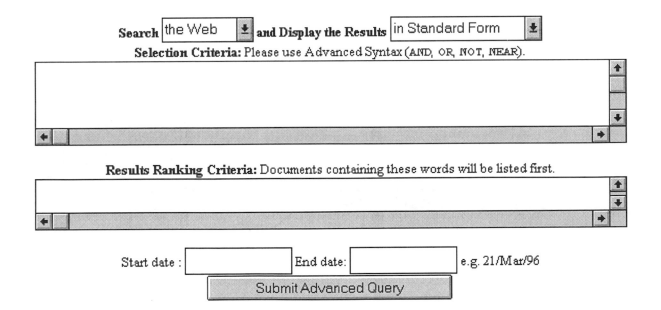

The *Advanced* interface has four command boxes. The first, labeled Selection Criteria, accepts the query statement. Below it lies the Results Ranking Criteria box for terms (usually some of the words from the Selection Criteria search statement) to be given highest weight in results ranking. Two small boxes lie below these, one for the beginning and one for the ending dates of a date-limited search. These restrict the search results to pages matching some range of dates. At the top of the page are the same pull-down menus as for the *Simple* search, offering the Web (default) or Usenet and the choice of the results display format. The only difference in the display choices from the *Simple* search is the option of displaying the search results as nothing but a numerical hit count, without the corresponding links. Although most of the help in creating a query is again left to separate Help pages, AltaVista includes a note that the query statement must contain at least one of the Boolean operators **AND**, **OR**, **NOT**, or **NEAR**.

AltaVista searches for words or terms, distinct from simple character strings. This prevents the user from retrieving pages containing the word **grants** when searching for **ants**. The user may search for phrases, either by placing the phrase in quotation marks or by putting punctuation of any kind between each word in the phrase. For example,

Search the Web ⬆ **and Display the Results** in Standard Form ⬆

"south america"   Submit

Tip: To find how many external pages point to a site you're interested in,
try: linkhttp://www.mysite.com -host:http://www.mysite.com
The minus sign before a word means that the word MUST NOT appear in the document.

would produce the same results as

Search the Web ⬆ **and Display the Results** in Standard Form ⬆

south.america   Submit

Tip: To find how many external pages point to a site you're interested in,
try: linkhttp://www.mysite.com -host:http://www.mysite.com
The minus sign before a word means that the word MUST NOT appear in the document.

or

Search the Web ⬆ **and Display the Results** in Standard Form ⬆

south/america   Submit

Tip: To find how many external pages point to a site you're interested in,
try: linkhttp://www.mysite.com -host:http://www.mysite.com
The minus sign before a word means that the word MUST NOT appear in the document.

Any type of punctuation will suffice to create a phrase. AltaVista treats punctuation marks like blank spaces in its index, simply as divisions that separate (and thus define) words. Searches are case sensitive, but only if the word in a search statement contains a capital letter. Search words all in lowercase letters will retrieve those words regardless of their case in the Web page, but if a word in the search statement contains a capital letter, the search is restricted to that exact formulation. For example,

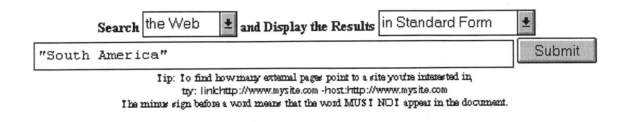

will return only those pages containing that exact capitalized phrase. On the other hand,

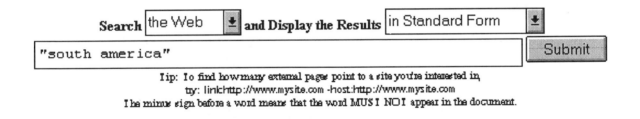

returns all of the pages that the capitalized version did, plus all pages with no capital letters and any variant capitalization, such as *souTH amerIca*. Numbers are treated the same as letters, so any combination of numbers and letters can be a query word.

Users may truncate the ends of search words with an asterisk to search for word roots, or place the asterisk inside the word to capture variant spellings and word forms. For example,

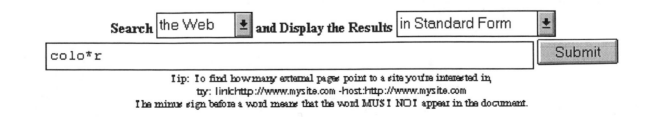

retrieves pages containing *color* and pages with *colour*. The asterisk must follow at least three characters of a word, however, or the word will be ignored in the search—neither *d*g* nor *fr*g* would be acceptable syntax. Also, the asterisk can only represent a maximum of five characters. Thus

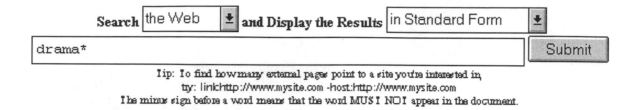

would not retrieve *dramatization*, since it extends eight characters beyond the initial word stem. Truncation symbols can only represent lowercase letters, not capital letters, numbers, or punctuation. For example *NAS** would not search for *NASA*, *Route** would not return *Route66*, and *computer** would not find *computer-based*. If the truncated search word pulls back "too many" hits, AltaVista ignores the term in computing results and tells the user no hits matched the term. We further address this problem below, in discussing AltaVista's method of ranking results.

AltaVista's *Simple* queries offer no Boolean operators, only plus (+) and minus (–) symbols which provide a weak approximation of them. If the user's *Simple* search contains nothing but several words, AltaVista effectively connects them with **OR**s. Such a search will return all Web pages in the index that contain any combination of one or more of the search words. If the user prefaces a query word with a plus sign, the search will retrieve only pages containing that word. The plus symbol approximates the Boolean **AND**. Similarly, a minus sign at the beginning of a word requires that the resulting pages **NOT** contain that word anywhere. For example,

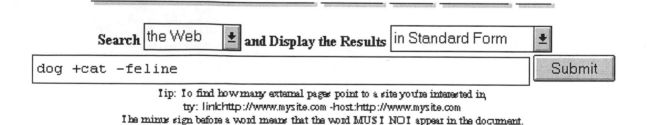

will find all Web pages in AltaVista's index containing the word *cat*, but not containing *feline*. The word "dog," since it does not have an operator, carries less weight than the words with operators. Given that the latter two words and their operators are more restrictive than the word *dog* with no operator, the presence of the word *dog* is ineffectual. There will probably be some pages in the results with the word *dog*, but all such pages would have to contain *cat* and omit *feline*. Conversely, many resulting pages will meet the latter two conditions, but not contain *dog* at all. Obviously, the plus sign is not the same as a typical Boolean *AND*, since the search statement

Search | the Web ⬍ | **and Display the Results** | in Standard Form ⬍

Selection Criteria: Please use Advanced Syntax (AND, OR, NOT, NEAR).

```
dog AND cat
```

in the *Advanced* AltaVista search option (or any other search engine recognizing Boolean *AND*) would require the resulting pages to contain both words. In our opinion this *Simple* search syntax is neither simple nor clear, particularly given the fact that the user must access separate Help pages to find even rudimentary examples of how to wield it. Novice users rarely bother to check the Help, nor do they consider the implications of its incomplete explanations. Experienced users would probably find the symbols misleading in their similarity to the corresponding traditional Boolean operators.

AltaVista's strength lies in its *Advanced* queries. Here the user can create query statements with common Boolean operators and punctuation. Truncation and phrase searching work in the same manner as in *Simple* queries. The available operators are *AND*, *OR*, *AND NOT*, and *NEAR*. These can be replaced by the symbols **&**, **/**, **!**, **~**, respectively. If *NOT* is the first operator in the query, it need not be preceded by *AND*. Thus

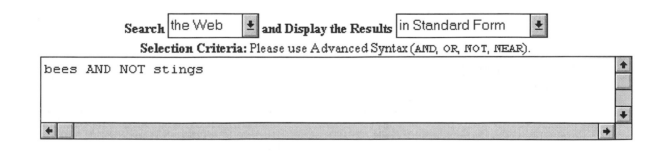

Search | the Web ⬍ | **and Display the Results** | in Standard Form ⬍

Selection Criteria: Please use Advanced Syntax (AND, OR, NOT, NEAR).

```
bees AND NOT stings
```

is equivalent to

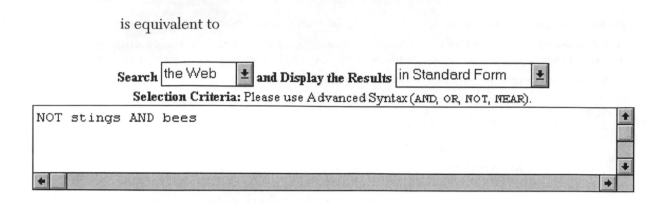

The user cannot specify the distance between terms when using **NEAR**. AltaVista automatically retrieves occurrences of words within ten words of one another. Thus

Search [the Web ▼] and Display the Results [in Standard Form ▼]
Selection Criteria: Please use Advanced Syntax (AND, OR, NOT, NEAR).

```
bees NEAR stings
```

retrieves pages where these words are separated by 0 to 10 other words. Also, the words need not occur in the order in which they appear in the query. Users may add parentheses to create more complex search statements in the usual manner.

As we mentioned, AltaVista indexes the full-text content of documents it encounters, plus positional information for each word in the document. One result is that users can restrict searches to pages where query words occur in particular areas or fields. Users must type field names in lower case, followed by a colon. The available fields include

For Web page searches

anchor: (matches pages with the user's phrase in the text of a
                 hyperlink)
applet: (matches pages with the user's phrase in the text of a Java
                 applet link)
host: (matches pages with the user's phrase in the host name of
                 the Web server)
image: (matches pages with the user's phrase in the text of an
                 image link)

link:	(matches pages with the user's phrase in the URL of a hyperlink within the page)
text:	(restricts phrase to body of the text the user sees)
title:	(matches pages with the user's phrase in the title field)
url:	(matches pages with the user's phrase in the page's URL)

For Usenet articles

from:	(restricts to the FROM field)
subject:	(restricts to the SUBJECT field)
newsgroups:	(restricts to articles posted to specified type of newsgroup)
summary:	(restricts to the SUMMARY field)
keywords:	(restricts to keyword list)

AltaVista appears to have no list of stopwords, at least not as they are traditionally defined. This makes sense, given that it claims to index the entirety of each page—to keep accurate word counts and position coordinates it could not toss out every occurrence of such high-frequency words as *and*, or *why*). In fact, one can search for any word in AltaVista, even the Boolean operators themselves (although they must be placed within quotation marks), but it is sometimes difficult to perform such a search and interpret the results, as we explain below.

RESULTS AND RANKING

AltaVista presents search results to the user in groups of ten. The user can jump to any of the first 20 such sets at any point by clicking on one of the numbers from 1 to 20 listed at the bottom of each page. This can be convenient, but there seems to be no way to reach any sets beyond 20 in the results of a *Simple* search. *Advanced* searches provide a *Next* choice to the user when he or she views hits 191–200. Yet *Simple* searches, no matter how many hits AltaVista says it has discovered, will present no more than 200 pages. Now, 200 hits may seem the most anyone would want to wade through, but the catch is that, since AltaVista may identify millions of hits, the user is dependent on the ranking process to get the right 200 out of the millions available. Unfortunately, ranking is not AltaVista's strength.

AltaVista uses ranking algorithms for ordering results sets, but provides no detail on how they work, except that the presence of user query words near the beginning of the Web page and multiple occurrences of query words throughout the document are the main determinants. Which of these factors carries more weight and how AltaVista treats varying degrees of occurrences across pages are just two pertinent questions we have been unable to answer.

AltaVista uses the same ranking method in both *Simple* and *Advanced* searches, but the actual results vary greatly depending on the user's chance to participate in the process. In *Advanced* queries, the user chooses which terms to enter into the Ranking Criteria box. If the ranking box is left empty, AltaVista does not rank the results at all. If the user enters words from the query into the ranking box, AltaVista ranks the results by moving to the top those pages that contain those terms in the headings, title, or first few lines; that have multiple occurrences of those terms; or that have query terms close to one another in the document. Again, AltaVista provides no details on how these factors influence page ranking. If the user enters words in the ranking box that were *not* part of the search statement, the engine discards those hits from the search results set that do not contain the ranking words. So, words in the ranking field *must occur* in *every* page in the results set, even if some of the ranking words were not part of the search.

For example, imagine the search statement is

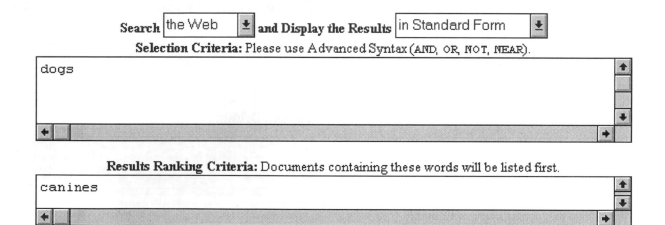

If 100 documents contain **dogs**, but no documents contain both **dogs** and **canines**, then the results set will be empty. If 20 of those 100 **dogs** documents contain **canines** as well, then those 20 alone will comprise the results set. AltaVista will rank those pages somehow, based on where and how often **canines** appears in each page, relative to the other pages.

AltaVista uses the same ranking algorithm for the results of *Simple* queries, but it automatically ranks the results using all of the words in the query, rather than allowing the user to pick the words by which to rank. Searchers cannot choose a subset of the terms for use in ranking, nor can they choose to skip ranking altogether. The novice user, however, gets the presumed benefit of ranking without having to know how to participate in the process. This would be more comforting if the workings of the algorithm itself were open to evaluation. This is yet one more reason to utilize AltaVista's *Advanced* query mode.

As we mentioned above, AltaVista does not treat as stopwords any words in its index or user queries. Even the Boolean operators are available for searching in *Advanced* queries, as long as they are bounded by quotation marks; however, in *Simple* searches, searching for an operator word with or without quotes returns an *"Ignored [#] No Results"* message. The same goes for traditional high-hit stopwords such as **be** and **who**. *Advanced* searches will return results with all of the words we have tried. The catch is that one cannot use the high-hit terms in the Ranking Criteria box.

A search on a single high-hit term such as **be** will return results, but the request to *rank* the results by this term will cause an error and retrieve no results. AltaVista is not up to the ranking task for so large a set. This explains the inevitable failure of these terms as searches in the *Simple* queries, since AltaVista automatically ranks *Simple* queries. *Simple* queries are treated as *Advanced* queries with the ranking box filled with all the terms of the query. When a high-hit term is used in a *Simple* search, AltaVista's attempt to rank with it fails. Even though the search may have retrieved a million hits, the user will not see any of them because of the ranking process's failure.

Thus the ranking process seems to be AltaVista's Achilles' heel. Granted, producing this failure requires an unlikely search query that few users may even try. Perhaps only a very small set of words, such as **why**, **and**, **be**—all commonly designated as stopwords—will trigger this error. But, since the set of such words is not available for the user to learn to avoid, and is not discarded from the query automatically, nor is the possibility of a failed search mentioned by AltaVista, it is easy to imagine a novice user creating a poor search statement that would trigger it. Such a user might well take the *"No Results"* message to mean that no documents on his topic are available. Further, liberal use of truncation in a query can also trigger this problem (although the Help file does warn of this error message in connection with truncation) since truncated word roots can retrieve so many hits.

Since we do not know the cutoff point for ranking problems (that is, the maximum number of hits AltaVista can rank), we can only warn users to respond to such errors with a trial-and-error strategy. The best method is to enter problem searches as *Advanced* queries with the ranking field left blank. Unfortunately this means these searches, probably with results in the millions, will not be ranked at all, making the resulting set of dubious value. The maximum number of hits returnable to the user is ten million, but if the user sets the display option to *Count Only*, AltaVista presents the actual number of documents matching the query.

Interestingly, this number is sometimes startlingly different from the number of estimated hits when the display form (for the same search query) is set for *Standard*, *Compact*, or *Detailed* results. The search

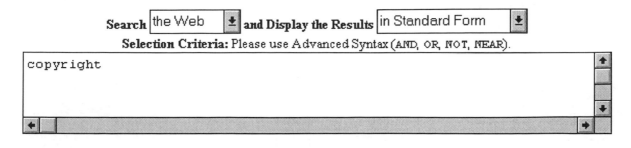

returned a hit count of 3.78 million, with the display set to *Count Only*; the same search produced "about 5000000" hits when the display was set to *Standard Form*. Even more curious, when we placed the term **copyright** in the ranking field, the results were "about 9000000" in *Standard Form* and 3.81 million with *Count Only*. These discrepancies do not occur with more manageable terms, such as **plato**, which AltaVista uses as an example in its Help pages. AltaVista only seems inconsistent with queries involving the most common words on the Web. This inconsistency may be more significant in the future, as the Web's rapidly increasing size pushes more and more terms into the realm of millions of hits, especially given AltaVista's reliance on its image as a brute-force word cruncher.

The biggest results set we have coaxed from AltaVista is one million hits, but if the display is set to *Count Only*, so that the actual links are not returned, there seems to be no limit. (The results are unavailable to check for accuracy, of course—but then who would examine 15 million links in detail?)

SUMMARY

All complaints aside, AltaVista usually beats its competitors in getting relevant hits ranked toward the top. Its advanced search interface is powerful and flexible (if a bit plain); its simple search should be avoided. It suffers in comparison to its competitors in that it lacks any useful reference tools besides its Web index, but for most searches it is first-rate.

NOTE

1.   AltaVista does not store each Web page as a file in its original form—you could not ask AltaVista to display the page as it would appear on the Web. Rather, AltaVista's index contains all the information necessary to reconstruct each page (that is, all of the words and where they lie in the page relative to one another).

*Pictures reproduced with the permission of Digital Equipment Corporation. AltaVista and the AltaVista logo and the Digital logo are trademarks of Digital Equipment Coporation.

Chapter 11

Excite

http://www.excite.com

HISTORY

Excite Web Search debuted for public use in late 1995. It is a product of Architext Software Corporation, a company formed in 1993 by six Stanford University students who wanted to create a search engine that offered an efficient way to perform concept searching on large databases. The Excite Web search site is a means of advertising the consequent searching and indexing software. Until August 1996 the software, Excite for Web Servers (EWS), was available for free from the Excite home page. Architext currently charges for EWS licenses. Webmasters may purchase it to index their own servers for local users' searches.

HOW EXCITE ADDS DOCUMENTS TO ITS DATABASE

Excite provides no information about its spider or its method of locating and harvesting documents. Authors may submit URLs of their Web pages so that Excite will visit them in its weekly run.

Excite claims to have indexed more than 50 million Web pages, as of February 1997. It gathers documents from at least three levels into a particular site, that is, the robot travels at least three levels of links on each server. Excite updates its index weekly. We tested the first ten hits of numerous different searches and found no dead links. Apparently the spider does a good job of checking for URL changes, keeping the index current. Excite does not seem to weight words in the index by their various HTML tags or other fields. Words in the <TITLE> field and URL seem to be treated equally to words in the body of the text. It does not recognize <META> tags. In addition, Excite does not track the relative position of the words in the documents it indexes. This eliminates the options of proximity and phrase searches found on other Web search tools (for example, WebCrawler and AltaVista).

Excite indexes HTML and ASCII text documents. Excite supposedly works with SGML (a broader mark-up language encompassing HTML) documents, although the company has not tested this. It plans to add PDF in later versions.

The key to Excite's concept searching function is the index. Excite uses an efficient form of Latent Semantic Indexing (LSI), called Intelligent Concept Extraction (ICE). LSI is based on the assumption that two documents on the same subject share many of the same words, even though they may use a variety of synonyms for the central concepts involved. LSI creates a kind of compressed, multiaxial index that groups related articles together, based on a clustering of words that often indicates the presence of like concepts. If a computer can identify and relate the documents through use of the language of the documents themselves, it can assume some of the functions of a thesaurus or classification system employed by human indexers. Assuming documents using similar words are related, computers can repeatedly identify and group documents by those relationships, on the fly—an enticing improvement over waiting for human thesaurus updates. The problem has been that this operation requires a huge amount of computing power, leaving LSI with little real-world testing or applications. Excite claims to have a more efficient approach. Unfortunately, in practice there seems to be little difference between Excite's concept searches and the more traditional keyword retrieval methods of other Web search tools.

Excite does not mention how it treats traditional stopwords when it indexes. By searching we have found that Excite omits the usual stopwords, such as *I*, *the*, *and*, *but*; such ubiquitous words as *computer* and *copyright*, however, are searchable. It appears that Excite discards a predefined set of words as it indexes documents, rather than automatically identify them based on their actual number of occurrences on the Web. But the list is not available to the user. Searches composed entirely of stopwords return an error message, saying that the word does not occur in the index. The query *To be or not to be* provoked such an error message. Sometimes traditional stopwords occurring in the search phrase seem to have an impact on the results, but we cannot find a common thread. A search for *The Rainmakers* gave us the same results set as a search for *Rainmakers*. Yet a search for *I Know Why the Caged Bird Sings* got us about 300,000 hits, when a search for *Know Why the Caged Bird Sings* gave us more than ten times that many.

Excite stores the full text of all the Usenet articles it harvests in its index. This feature allows the user to link directly to an article if it shows up on the results list, whether or not the local newsgroup server carries that group.

INTERFACE AND SEARCHING

The Excite search interface is a single command line. The simple or advanced nature of the search is determined by the user's search syntax—whether the user enters a natural language query or a simple list of words, or words connected with one or more operators. A pull-down menu below the command line lets users choose what to search (the Web, Usenet, or Excite Reviews).

Concept searching is what Architext Software advertises it does. Architext claims that user search terms need not actually appear in a page for Excite to identify the page as a concept match. For example, if you searched for **automobiles** in a concept search, you would get some pages that do not actually contain that word, but words that are conceptually related to **automobiles,** like **cars, vans, trucks**, and **Toyotas**.

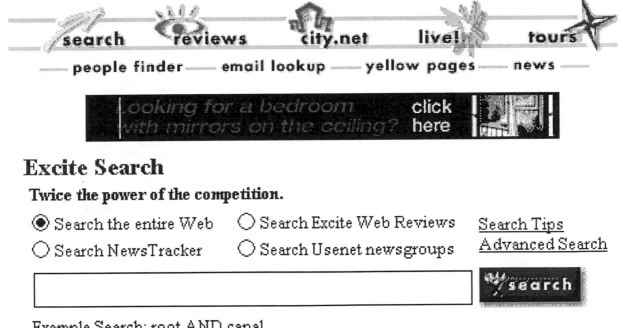

Excite's Help documentation consists primarily of tips on syntax and how to use special features. It offers no discussion of how weighting or other features work. It does, however, provide inaccurate definitions of *recall* and *precision*, as well as poor descriptions of Boolean and vector searching techniques.

SEARCH FEATURES AND OPERATORS

If the user's search contains nothing but several keywords, Excite automatically connects them with Boolean **OR**. Thus, Excite searches by default for any combination of one or more query terms within a page; however, documents containing all of the search words (that is, those documents that would be retrieved by **AND**ing all of the search words) are presented first in the results set due to the ranking algorithm. These are followed by the rest of the documents that contain any of the search terms, in order of decreasing frequency of occurrences in the page. Assuming that documents with all of the search words are more relevant than documents with just some (or one), the user gets the completeness of an **OR** search with the "best" results first. Excite refers to this approach as "fuzzy AND."

Users can place some constraints on words in a simple query. Preceding a word with a plus sign (**+**) forces Excite to return only those pages containing that word. A minus sign (**-**) in front of a word tells Excite to omit pages containing that word. For example,

Excite Search
Twice the power of the competition.

◉ Search the entire Web   ◯ Search Excite Web Reviews   Search Tips
◯ Search NewsTracker   ◯ Search Usenet newsgroups   Advanced Search

`+bees honey -wax`   [search]

would return all pages in Excite's index containing **bees** that do not contain **wax**. The plus operator renders the word **honey** in the search statement moot, in terms of retrieval. Since Excite will retrieve all pages with **bees** and only pages with **bees**, and does not require **honey** to appear in the pages (because **honey** was not preceded by a plus sign), **honey** plays no role in retrieval; however, **honey** will be incorporated into the ranking process, pushing those pages containing both words toward the top of the list. Unfortunately, Excite claims that this plus operator performs the same function as the Boolean **AND** operator. This is not true. The plus operator applies to single words—**AND** applies to words or phrases on both sides of it. Consequently,

Excite Search

Twice the power of the competition.

⦿ Search the entire Web   ○ Search Excite Web Reviews   Search Tips

○ Search NewsTracker   ○ Search Usenet newsgroups   Advanced Search

```
bees AND honey -wax
```
[search]

would produce different results from the previous search, since it would require that the pages retrieved contain both **bees** and **honey**. In this second form, **honey** becomes as important as **bees** in defining the results set. To replicate this in Excite with the plus operator would require

Excite Search

Twice the power of the competition.

⦿ Search the entire Web   ○ Search Excite Web Reviews   Search Tips

○ Search NewsTracker   ○ Search Usenet newsgroups   Advanced Search

```
+bees +honey -wax
```
[search]

Excite does offer advanced searching using **AND** and other Boolean operators. The syntax is described in the Advanced Search Options link. The available operators are **AND**, **OR**, **AND NOT**, and **NOT**. The user may connect keywords with these operators, but they must be typed in all capital letters. For example, the search

Excite Search: twice the power of the competition.

What:
```
NHL and hockey
```
[search]

Where:
```
World Wide Web        ▼
```
[Help]
[Add URL]

retrieves more than 300,000 hits, while the search

Excite Search: twice the power of the competition.

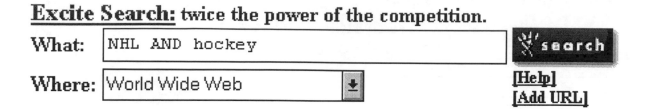

gives the user 24,000 hits.

Excite also allows parentheses in an advanced search statement. For example, if the user is looking for *curriculum* for an elementary classroom, the following search statement would find all documents in the database that contain *elementary* and *curriculum*, or *primary* and *curriculum*, but exclude all pages with the term *secondary*:

(elementary OR primary) AND curriculum NOT secondary

When ranking results, Excite does not weight terms based on their position in the document. A page with a search term in its HTML <TITLE> field is treated the same as a page with the same word in the body of the text. Users may, however, weight one query term over another by using it more than once in the search statement. Alternatively, following the word with a circumflex (^) and a number does the same thing. For example, the following search statements would rank pages containing the word *Dublin* and not *Ireland* higher than pages with *Ireland* and not *Dublin*.

Excite Search: twice the power of the competition.

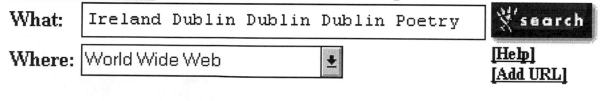

Excite Search: twice the power of the competition.

Excite searches for text strings, not words. The difference for the user is in the scope of the results retrieved. Searching for any occurrence of a text string retrieves larger sets of results. For example,

Excite Search: twice the power of the competition.

What: `arm bone`

Where: `World Wide Web`   [search]

[Help]
[Add URL]

will retrieve all of the following words (among others): *arm*, *armed*, *arms*, *farm*, *farms*, *harm*, *swarm*, *swarms*, *bone*, *trombones*. In other words, every term in the query is automatically truncated both to the left and right. Excite has no truncation operator for the user to add to a word. Consequently, although most plurals and verb cases are covered automatically, the user must account for alternate spellings (such as *color/colour*, *mouse/mice*) by including each variation in the query.

Excite is not case sensitive, except to Boolean operators and persons' names. Name searches require that the user capitalize both the first and last names. If the name is part of a multiple word search statement, it must be separated from the rest of the keywords by quotation marks or parentheses (for example, *government "Bill Clinton"*). Excite ignores punctuation (other than plus and minus signs, circumflex, quotation marks, and parentheses) and dates.

RESULTS AND RANKING

Excite's search results are lists of page links and summaries, which can be sorted by *confidence* or by *site*. The default is sorting by confidence, but a button at the beginning of the list enables the user to choose sorting by site. The confidence list is sorted by a ranking algorithm, which Excite does not describe. Presumably this ranking process incorporates any weights that the user may have attached to query words. Excite gives each link in the results a percentage score from 99% to 1%. No document receives a 100% score, unless it was used to launch a *Query by Example* search, in which case it is automatically the first hit in the results with a 100% score. Each link has an automatically generated summary of the document. Excite creates the summaries using its LSI techniques. Once Excite indexes a document and determines its position in the concept spaces of its index, it searches the document for two or three sentences most representative of the dominant concept(s). It then extracts those sentences and uses them as a *de facto* summary. The assumption is that this method allows the user to make a more accurate comparison between links in the results page than the more common method of generating summaries from the first few lines of the pages. In addition, the ads in the results sets are keyed to particular user search terms. For instance, a search on **computer** may present the user with an IBM banner ad across the top and bottom of the page.

The results by site option (not available in Usenet searches) displays results as a list of HTML <TITLE>s, with no summaries. Excite groups <TITLE> links together by the Web servers on which they reside. Documents that live on the same machine are listed next to one another, rather than being individually ordered by the ranking algorithm. This option can be very useful. For example, if a given server is too busy or unavailable for some reason, the user can quickly ignore the entire group of documents from that location and move on to another. Likewise, if the user finds an especially useful document on a given server, chances are good that it is a reflection of other documents on the server. The user can quickly test this and either take advantage of a ready pool of resources, or determine that the relevant document is a fluke and go elsewhere. Also, users can take better advantage of institutions with known reputations. For instance, all the pages on Arterial Venous Malformation residing on the National Library of Medicine's server would be together, along with the authority of the site they share. (Keep in mind that for important information needs, such as medical questions, the searcher *must* trust the source of information—that is, judge it to be a recognized authority; this trust can be difficult to establish in the Web environment.) This method also cuts down on user attempts to follow duplicate links to the same information, which would otherwise be scattered throughout the results set by the ranking process.

The use of the fuzzy **AND** search as the default creates a relatively large results set, especially with concept searching; however, the total number of hits is often meaningless, since every article in Excite's database could be related to any given user search via shared text. Getting a results set numbering in the millions is common. Using the fuzzy **AND** search, Excite looks first for documents containing all the keywords associated with the concepts, not just the keywords in the user's query. It then drops one concept and looks for those documents containing only two of the concepts, then only one. The ranking algorithm measures the likelihood of a particular document relating to the user request. Pages containing only one concept rank near the bottom of the list. Neither Excite nor the user is likely to be interested in the bottom one-half million hits of a ranked search, so the hit count is not expected to be a useful measure.

A user who finds the perfect page in the results of a query can click the *Query by Example* icon to the left of the link. Excite will create a new query based on words occurring in that page. Excite extracts words from the document and transforms them into concept searches, using the ICE methods mentioned above. Overall the results from this feature are uneven, as they are for similar features offered by other search tools.

Excite also attempts to cluster subgroups of similar documents within the results set, a method it calls *Automatic Subject Grouping*. This feature is "an added benefit of Excite's ICE searching." The idea is that the ICE approach automatically recognizes clusters of documents by identifying shared "separable concepts." The example Excite provides in its documentation is a search for ***bonds***.[1] This search should retrieve a set of results with groups of pages discussing chemical bonds, groups about psychological bonds, and groups offering municipal bonds. Surprisingly, when we performed this search for ***bonds***, the top ten hits grouped inconsistently as follows:

1	Financial
2	Barry Bonds (athlete)
3–7	Financial
8	Atomic Bonds
9	Financial
10	Bail Bonds in Oklahoma

As before, the ICE magic does not quite live up to Excite's hype.

SUMMARY

Excite's ICE technology offers a great opportunity for automatic indexing. The ability to create relationships on the fly between documents might eventually lead to decent indexing of the Web. Unfortunately, in practice, we could not find much difference between Excite and other Web search tools. Excite generally gives users something related to their search terms in the first ten to 20 hits. But Excite's underlying processes (such as stemming, weighting, conceptual relation) are hidden from the user. Excite may automatically perform phrase and proximity searches, or approximate them with ICE, but it never tells the user. Anemic Help files do not help matters. Excite only truly shines in its presentation of search results, where the *sort by site* option offers a great opportunity to avoid duplicates and mine useful servers.

NOTE

1. Information Retrieval Technology and Intelligent Concept Extraction Searching: A Technology Backgrounder from Excite, Inc. 1996 (http://www.excite.com/ice/tech.html).

Chapter 12

HotBot

http://www.hotbot.com

HISTORY

Inktomi Corporation and HotWired (publisher of *Wired* magazine) sponsor the HotBot search tool. Inktomi was formed in early 1996 by assistant professor of computer science Dr. Eric Brewer and Ph.D. candidate in computer science Paul Gauthier of the University of California at Berkeley. The name Inktomi refers to the Plains Indians trickster spider, a Promethean figure who brought culture to the people.

HotBot demonstrates Inktomi's networking and indexing software products. HotBot's angle on indexing the Web is parallel processing (that is, linking multiple computer "brains" together to share a heavy workload). HotBot links a number of typical PCs and workstations into what it calls *a Network of Workstations* (NOW), sort of a souped-up local area network (LAN). In theory this method gives HotBot the ability to combine the resources of indefinite numbers of small, cheap computers to produce an index much larger than each could create on its own. Since PCs are cheap and HotBot can add more to the network as they are needed, this strategy provides a means for HotBot to try to keep up with the growing Web. This also means that if one of the PCs crashes, the rest of its siblings in the network can pick up the slack, so that the user does not suffer. So far as we can tell, HotBot's strategy works as well as those of its competitors.

Audience1 is the other Inktomi software program marketed through HotBot. Audience1 allows HotBot to customize its interaction to match each user's browser. HotBot can target advertising by changing ad formats to fit each browser's abilities. Newer browsers will recognize frames and Java, while older browsers display still images or regular text.

HOW HOTBOT ADDS DOCUMENTS TO ITS DATABASE

HotBot claims to be the "fastest crawler" on the Web, indexing over seven million documents a week, for a total of 54 million by February 1997. HotBot expects its spider, Slurp, will update every page of its index each week. While testing the engine, we received only one dead link in all of the searches we performed, suggesting that the index is indeed very up-to-date. Slurp honors the robot exclusion protocol. To reduce the number of duplicates in its index, it also recognizes and notes duplicate pages it encounters on the Web, but only with mixed results. HotBot indexes most of the words in each page Slurp delivers and recognizes a variety of document formats, including VRML (Virtual Reality Modeling Language), Java, and the requisite HTML.

INTERFACE AND SEARCHING

HotBot omits some common stopwords from its index (for example, *of* and *the*) but keeps others (for example, *but* and *why*), with no list available to the user. The index does keep track of the relative position in a page of each word it indexes, but because HotBot leaves out stopwords, these positions are inexact. HotBot also recognizes and utilizes the HTML <TITLE> tag and the subject <META> tags to help it rank search results. HotBot does index international character sets, but viewing them in the results depends on the user's browser's ability to display multiple character sets.

The screen is typically three-fourths search options, with the top quarter of the page devoted to third-party advertisements. The search interface contains five sections: *Search, Modify, Date, Location,* and *Media Type*. The *Search* section consists of one command line for entering search terms, a pull-down menu with six options for linking the search terms (*all of the words, any of the words, the exact phrase, the person, links to this URL,* and *the Boolean expression*), two pull-down menus for picking the number of hits (10, 25, 40, 75 or 100) and format (full description, brief description, or URLs only), and a button icon for submitting the search. The *Modify, Date, Location,* and *Media Type* areas of the search interface are optional; the user can add or delete these sections by clicking on their labels. Be aware, however, that some browsers cannot display these features—in fact much of the site is inaccessible or problematic for some browsers, a drawback of HotBot's infatuation with flashy new features. The default view is simply the *Search* section.

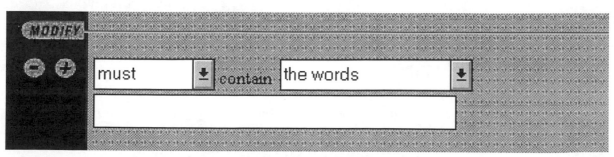

Users must add the optional sections of a HotBot search page one at a time, since each addition requires downloading a new page from the HotBot server. This process can take a while; thus HotBot allows the frequent user to save an ideal search page on his or her own hard drive, to be loaded each time he or she uses HotBot. The user need only create a page with a favorite number of options enabled and click the *Save My Settings* button. From then on, with each use of HotBot (from the same PC) his or her version of the HotBot search page will appear (although with some browsers it is necessary to click the *Load My Settings* button at the bottom of the page). HotBot is pushing this customization feature heavily, in part because it helps HotBot to customize advertising by storing users' preferences (or at least the preferences of the people using the same machine).

The optional *Modify* section allows the searcher to add or subtract additional command lines and menus to link them, for adding more terms to the search. A click on the plus (+) or minus (-) signs below the word *modify* adds or subtracts command lines one at a time.

Two drop-down menus provide operators for a *Modify* command line, but they must be used together. The first menu offers *must contain*, *should contain*, and *must not contain*. The second menu, just to the right of the first, has four options for completing those three phrases: *the words*, *the exact phrase*, *the person*, and *links to this URL*.

The optional *Date* section allows the user to limit the search by date. The date search only checks when HotBot *found* a given page; it does *not* search the date the document was created, last modified, or placed on the Web.

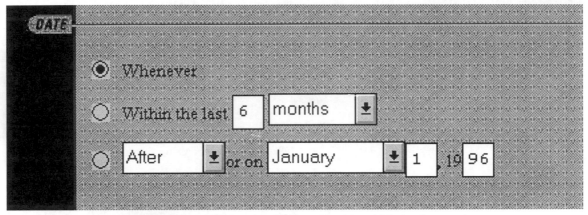

The user may ask for pages HotBot found "whenever" (the default), before or after a specific date, or within the last user-specified number of years, months, or days.

The optional *Location* section limits by the domain code (such as *.com*, *.edu*, and *.uk*) in a Web page's URL. The *AnyPlace* box does not limit the search by location at all. The *CyberPlace* option provides a command line where users may enter any domain codes. For example, typing *.uk* would limit a search to pages harvested from servers in the United Kingdom; *.edu* would limit to pages from educational facilities in the United States (note: domain codes begin with a period).

The *GeoPlace* option provides a convenient shortcut for restricting searches to large geographic regions. A drop-down menu provides choices (such as *North America*, *Europe*, *Oceania*), each of which represents a predefined set of domain codes associated with the given region. Using our previous examples, *North America* would encompass *.com* and *.edu*, while *.uk* would fall under *Europe*. Users can define their own regions in a search by typing more than one domain code into the *CyberPlace* command line, separating each with a space. Such a search would retrieve only pages whose URLs contain one of the user's specified domain codes.

The optional *Media Type* section contains a variety of check-boxes which restrict search results to pages incorporating multimedia files. It does *not* search for pages *about* specific media types (for example, checking the *Java* box will not retrieve pages on how to program with Java). Instead, checking a media type box instructs HotBot to look for pages containing filenames whose file extensions (such as *.html* and *.htm* which often punctuate Web page filenames) identify that type of media. For example, checking the *Image* box would restrict a search to pages containing filenames that end with *.gif* or other standardized image file format codes. HotBot provides check-boxes for a variety of common formats (*Java, JavaScript, Audio, Acrobat, Shockwave, VRML,* and *Image*), as well as a command line for users to search for others.

HotBot's Help documentation is a mixed bag. Clicking on the Help button links the user to a page with two options. The *How to Use HotBot* link connects the user to a Java-based page containing a miniature version of the *Search* page, with each of its features labeled. Clicking on a label produces a brief description of the feature in a second frame along the bottom of the screen. For instance, clicking on the *Modify* button explains how to add or remove additional command lines to modify a search, while the illustration of the search page remains in view above it. Although the format of this Help screen is exceptionally clear and informative, it is too complicated for some browsers to display. In fact, as late as February 1997, the Java components of the Help display contained bugs that rendered it unusable on some of our Netscape 3.0 and 4.0 browsers. The other link on the Help page connects the user to the FAQ list. This is one of the more detailed search tool FAQs we have seen so far; however, the FAQ does not cover all of the information within the Java-based *How to Use HotBot*, leaving at a distinct disadvantage those users without the ability to access both.

HotBot does accept Boolean operators and punctuation in the *Search* section command line, but only if the user chooses *the Boolean expression* option in the drop-down menu. Otherwise, HotBot treats Boolean operators as stopwords and simply links keywords according to the user's choice from the menu. Choosing the *all of the words* option will only retrieve pages containing all of the keywords, while the *any of the words* option will retrieve any pages with one or more of the keywords. To approximate Boolean **NOT** and exclude a term from the search results (without choosing *the Boolean expression* option), the user must add extra command lines in the *Modify* section, discussed below.

Also on the pull-down menu, *the exact phrase* option searches for the exact words of the query in the order they appear (just like quotation marks in a Boolean expression). Since HotBot does not index some stopwords (such as **of, the**), it treats them as wildcards in a phrase query. We found that phrases incorporating stopwords produce spotty results, especially if the user is looking for a natural language quote. Spoken text and narrative prose tend to be littered with stopwords, leading to multiple false hits in the search results. For example, this feature is very useful when searching for **rock and roll**, since it will retrieve **rock and roll**, **rock 'n' roll**, **rock & roll**, and so on. HotBot retrieves phrases that contain any word in the stopword's position in the user query; however, it is a disastrous feature when searching for **to be or not to be**, which does not work at all. Such searches, composed entirely of stopwords, produce no results. HotBot simply ignores stopwords occurring in searches other than phrase searches.

If the user enters a two- or three-word query, choosing *the person* option from the pull-down menu performs a limited proximity search modeled on three common name formats. HotBot searches for a two-word name like Mark Twain with **Mark Twain** and **Twain, Mark**. It searches a three-word name like Brett Easton Ellis as **Brett Easton Ellis**, **Brett Ellis**, and **Ellis, Brett**. The latter search will also retrieve pages with **Ellis, Brett Easton** by default, since it begins with **Ellis, Brett**.

The user can also apply the person search for very strict proximity searching on two or three subject terms in the same manner. For example,

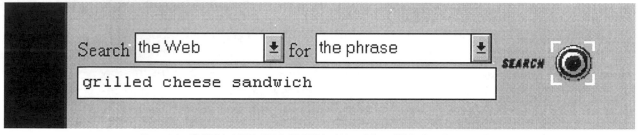

would retrieve **grilled cheese sandwich**; **sandwich, grilled**; and **grilled sandwich**. HotBot plans to offer a more powerful proximity search in the future.

The *Links to this URL* option restricts searches to keywords within URLs that appear in the body of a page. In other words, the Web pages in the results set may not contain any keywords from the search—but somewhere within the bodies of those pages are URLs that do.

The operators in the *Modify* menus relate the search terms in the associated command line to the rest of the search (that is, the main *Search* area and any additional *Modify* lines), much like the menu in the *Search* area. Choosing *Must contain* in the first menu and *the words* option in the second menu restricts results to pages containing all of the user's keywords, just like the *all the words* option in the *Search* area. The *Should* option does not require that query words appear in the results page (just like the *Search* area's *any of the words* option), but it does cause HotBot to rank pages with the words higher than those without them. The *Must not* option (which has no counterpart in the *Search* area) works like Boolean **NOT**, returning only pages that do not contain the keywords. If the user chooses either *the exact phrase, the person*, or *Links to this URL* (instead of *the words* option) in the second menu, HotBot looks for phrases, names, or URLs as we described earlier. The only difference between the *Search* area and the *Modify* area is that the latter provides a *Must not* option. Oddly enough, *Modify* command lines containing search terms will work even if the main *Search* command line (which the user is presumably modifying) is empty.

HotBot does not offer truncation or wildcard search operators. Since it searches for words and not just character strings, the user must type plural forms and alternate spellings of keywords to get a thorough search. For example, the search **insect** retrieves only half as many hits as the search **insect insects** using the *any of the words* option.

HotBot is not case sensitive, for the most part. The exceptions are words that HotBot describes as having "interesting case" (for example, words like **NeXT**, **XeroX**, and **HotBot**), which mix lowercase and uppercase in unusual ways. One of the most interesting things about interesting case is its popularity among the names and logos of advertisers and corporate sponsors.

RESULTS AND RANKING

Directly below the command line in the *Search* section, two menus determine the number and format of search results. Users may choose to receive 10, 25, 50, 75, or 100 hits in each page of results, as well as request hits as full or brief descriptions, or URLs only. If the user chooses 100 hits per result page, the page takes quite a bit longer to load, but it can be much more convenient than shuffling between ten pages with ten hits each. Full descriptions include a hot-linked title, a weak summary (automatically generated by HotBot from the first few lines of text), URL, file size (in bytes), and the date the page was harvested. Brief descriptions include only the title link and first line of the summary. Each hit in the results set is prefaced by a percentage from 1 to 99 that reflects HotBot's normalized ranking score for that page.

HotBot frequently describes its results ranking algorithm as "prizewinning." Although HotBot and Inktomi provide little detail, the ranking does involve a ratio of the query words' frequencies in a document to the overall document length. For example, if a word from the user's search appears twice in a one-page document and twice in a 1,000 page document, the former will be ranked higher than the latter. Pages containing user terms in the HTML <TITLE> tag and <META> tags are given considerably more weight than pages with the words only in the body of the text. All of these weights are used to some degree and in various combinations in other Web search tools reviewed in this book. Using the ratio of term occurrence to overall document length is problematic, since long texts on a specific subject tend to employ more synonyms and other vocabulary related to the subject than do short texts. This can lead HotBot to an unwelcome bias for short documents. HotBot does ask for feedback from users who receive odd results.

Possibly the most useful aspect of HotBot's results sets is that it clusters identical documents. When HotBot discovers another copy on the Web of a document it has already indexed under a different URL, it sends the user only one link, with the other alternate links underneath the summary. The alternates are included in the document count, so a document with three alternate URLs listed will count as four in the total number of hits. This lessens the irritating problem for users of continually accessing the same document as they go through the results. For example,

6.   🖻 Sandwich Menu

97% Ruggles Sandwich on Grilled Sourdough...$7.95 w/ Grilled Chicken Breast, Sauteed Mushrooms, Avocado, Sour Cream & Fontina Cheese Grilled Seasonal Vegetable Sandwich...$5.95 w/ Roasted...

http://www.insync.net/houston/dineH/ruggles/sandwich.html, 1622 bytes, 07Jun96

7. (alternate)
http://www.dineusa.com/houston/dineH/restaurants/ruggles/sandwich.html, 1622 bytes, 16Nov95

8. (alternate)
http://www.insync.net/houston/dineH/restaurants/ruggles/sandwich.html, 1622 bytes, 03Oct95

This feature usually works well, but sometimes HotBot misses the duplicates and the user gets more than one link. The search

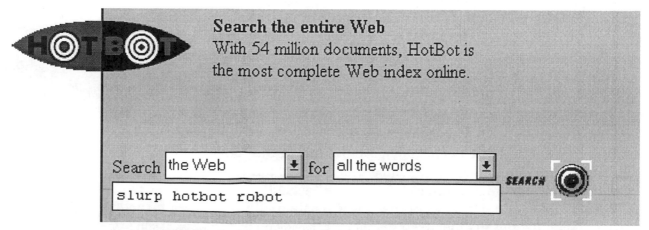

produced 33 hits, of which five of the first ten links were duplicates.

SUMMARY

Overall HotBot is better than most of the Web search tools at ranking the best results at the top. Furthermore, it is one of the most comprehensive indexes of the Web. We never encountered a maximum hit limit in search results, although the biggest set we retrieved (using *web*) was about 5.5 million. Its interface is eye-catching and more powerful than most (especially since it added Boolean searching), but cumbersome, especially if the user does not set up a default form. Worst of all, HotBot's interface is the most unfriendly to old or text-only browsers, rendering many search options and the Help inaccessible to some users. Also, the voluminous third-party advertising is often distracting (although admittedly that is its purpose). If HotBot paid more attention to usability than visibility, it would probably be the best tool around.

SECTION IV

WEB SEARCH TOOLS IN CONTEXT

Chapter 13

The Economics of Web Search Tools

Commercial Web search tools presently have two major methods of generating revenue: selling advertising space, and selling the robot software for use on corporate intranets. An obvious third method is charging users for the privilege of searching and retrieving results, either with a fee for each transaction or a subscription for unlimited access; however, this is not likely to develop into a viable option for Web indexes. Where Dialog and other commercial database vendors provide heavily manipulated and carefully chosen content (and generate tremendous amounts of money), tools that index the Web are providing automated discovery and indexing of a hodgepodge collection of documents. The Web is currently too shallow and chaotic a source—and robotic indexing of it too unreliable—for Web search tools to charge a significant amount for usage. Infoseek initially charged users for search results. Before long it began offering free searches of its Web index, while maintaining separate fee-based searching of proprietary databases. By the fall of 1996, Infoseek had abandoned even this secondary fee-based service.

Even though the fee-based model is the historical precedent for commercial databases in other environments, Web indexes have not proven themselves worth a fee to their primary audience. Librarians and other professional online database searchers comprise the traditional customer base for fee-for-use database providers such as Dialog. The vast majority of Web users, however, do not search the Web for a living (especially with their jobs hanging on the quality of the results). In fact, neither do most professional searchers (although this is already changing, as original research and other valuable information gradually appears on the Web). Web search tools do not yet provide essential content with a quality to match that of traditional fee-based vendors. Obviously, this is not to imply that they are not valuable, just not worth paying for.

Most of the search tools already sell ad space and software. Open Text is the only tool we have discussed that does not accept third-party advertisers (although it did until early 1997). The rest charge advertisers a flat rate, either for the number of times a hotlinked banner advertisement is displayed, or for the number of clicks an ad draws to its associated company home page. On the other hand, WebCrawler is the only one that does not sell its robot index-building and searching software. In particular, the other search tools market their entire package of components as tools for corporate intranets. Customers may purchase the discovery and harvesting robots to find and centrally index documents inhabiting their corporate intranet and/or the Internet; the same search engine software is sold to search the resulting indexes; and browsers and CGI applications provide a user interface. By offering free searching, Web tools provide a chance to display this software to their audience of potential customers, just as they display ads for third-party products and services.

What makes Open Text and WebCrawler different? Open Text is currently a showpiece for its parent company's products (intranet software), like most of the other search engines, but Open Text has decided to use the screen space typically sold to third-party advertisers to advertise its own product exclusively. Given that Open Text formerly sold space to other advertisers, one could take it as a sign that search engine ad revenue may not be very lucrative after all, at least as long as the company has its own ad costs to consider. On the other hand, maybe Open Text was simply selling fewer ads than its competitors, or needs to use every available avenue to catch up in the race to supply corporate intranets. At the moment, WebCrawler serves as a sample of the services available from America OnLine (which purchased it in 1995). Unlike the other search tools, whose producers became incorporated in order to market their search tools, WebCrawler was purchased by an established commercial organization to be a walking, talking ad for something else. So far AOL does not seem inclined to develop and sell the WebCrawler technology as a consumer product. In fact, rumors already suggest that AOL is considering dumping WebCrawler. If so, this would suggest that Web search tools have been over-hyped as customer lures.

Web search tools have proven successful in selling advertising space. Advertising represented the largest portion of the revenue generated over the Web during the first half of 1996. As of August 1996, four of the top ten ad-selling Web sites were search engines, and Yahoo! was one of the remaining six.

So far most ad sales have been based on the number of guaranteed *viewings*. In this model, the search site guarantees that the customer's ad will appear on computer screens in front of users a certain number of times, in exchange for a fixed amount of money. So, if you see a Toyota ad on ten different occasions while using OpenText, it fulfills about $.05 of OpenText's commitment to Toyota. A competing model bases charges on the number of times users click on an ad and visit the corporate page to which it is linked, rather than the number of times users *see* the ad. Obviously, this model is not what the search tool producers would prefer—only a very small percentage of users click on banner ads, compared to the number who see them. To make as much money, the search tool would have to provide more incentive for the user to follow an ad link, or charge the advertiser more for each click than each viewing. However, Procter & Gamble already demanded and received such a deal from Yahoo!

An increasingly popular advertising twist ties a company banner to a particular keyword in the search tool's Web index. Every time a user searches with the keyword, the company's ad will appear at the top of the results page. For example, a search for *dogs* might elicit a banner ad for Purina dog food, along with the search results. This strategy allows advertisers to improve their chances of reaching a likely customer. Other innovative strategies will become standard practice in the near future if commercial Web search tools are to survive, especially since many advertisers are already beginning to wonder if their returns justify their spending.

FUTURE OPTIONS

Third-party advertising on the Web has not been around long enough to evaluate accurately. Some industry watchers are predicting ad revenues will skyrocket in 1997 and continue to rise through the year 2000. In spite of the mass media's hyperbolic enthusiasm for the Web, which threatens to raise new users' expectations to heights the real experience could never match, use is rapidly increasing. Nevertheless, advertisers will be watching closely for signs that the entire phenomenon is a fad or simply a poor advertising media, to make sure they are not throwing money down a hole. No matter the outcome, we suspect that the major search tools will want to continue to look for other sources of income.

Some search tools may be tempted to try a more distasteful means of advertising, by selling positions in user search results. Sort of the evil stepsister to tying banner ads to keywords, this approach would basically make profit a factor in the ranking algorithms. An advertiser could purchase the ensurance that if a user search retrieved its Web page from the index, it would automatically receive a high position in the user's results page. One or two major Web search tools are rumored to have at least considered this option, but none admit to participating in such a scheme. Authors often try to influence ranking by repeating one or two keywords over and over in the initial text of a Web page, since search tools tend to factor into the ranking equation the number of times a keyword appears in a page. Several search tools refuse to index such pages, by programming their robots to try to identify and ignore them. We hope these tools do not decide to turn around and pull similar tricks on their users by inflating the ranking of their advertisers' pages.

WebCrawler's relationship with AOL could prove to be a popular model for other Web search tools (although, if that relationship is indeed already souring as speculated, it may well not). All of these tools have garnered a lot of attention (WebCrawler was just more established and more available when AOL came a-courtin') and AOL does not have the deepest pockets in the online community. Many of the tools we have covered now advertise themselves as the official search engines of a variety of other companies. Many Web pages feature Infoseek and

Excite command lines, search forms, and logos. Yahoo! automatically passes user searches to AltaVista when it cannot answer them. Rather than having an ad on the search tools' home and results pages, these companies put the engine on their own site, in the hopes of drawing users closer. Although this is a far cry from owning the search tool, *à la* AOL and WebCrawler, it is still a closer relationship than the current banner ads model (and it gives the search tools more exposure to visitors of other sites). New partnerships will fill some gaps left by banner ad revenues.

It is still possible for nonprofit and educational institutions, especially universities and research groups, to regain strong presences in Web searching. WebCrawler, Lycos, and HotBot all began as projects by graduate students and computer science departments. Such institutions might continue to be the launching pad for new generations of search tools, even if they all go commercial eventually. Yet none of the present generation of commercial engines will be returning to their educational roots, except perhaps to buy innovations. Further, all of these tools have significant leads on upstart rivals—large indexes of Web pages, which inevitably require lots of time and money to create. Future nonprofit projects will have to incorporate increasingly innovative and powerful technology in order to compete for popular attention.

The most likely scenario is that the current crop of search tools will continue to expand their portfolios of services and products, to spread their eggs among more than one basket. Ad revenues will probably continue to grow, although the rate and duration of this growth are highly debatable. Since most of these tools have already begun selling their component software, they will probably continue to focus on this commitment (barring failure to sell anything). Consequently, much of their resources will go into improving, expanding, and marketing these products. One must wonder, however, how much of this innovation will actually improve the free public versions of these search tools, especially if brand loyalty (which is based primarily on *past* accomplishments) becomes a more potent force for luring customers.

If the increasing size of the Web proves to be too much for general search tools to handle well, it seems likely that smaller tools will arise that will seek to add more value to specific pieces of the Web. As we have seen, searching the general tools routinely produces results sets with many thousands of hits. As the problem worsens, smaller tools may woo users by focusing on and doing a better job with small subsets of the Web. Users tired of wading through dozens of irrelevant hits could instead search an index that provides more sophisticated retrieval of Web documents with a common subject. The large general tools might decide to downsize and focus their efforts, rather than expand their services. The problem with this scenario is that the more specialized the tool becomes, the more specialized are the needs it can conceivably satisfy. Specialized tools will draw a smaller audience (or at least fewer searches), since they are designed for specific needs. This limits such a tool's appeal to advertisers, making it more difficult to generate revenue.

Besides software and ad space, search tools may soon begin selling another valuable commodity—demographic information and the search habits of their users. We mentioned earlier that several search tools already tie ads to specific keywords, in an attempt to target advertising to specific users. In a similar move, search tools will begin keeping track of the topics that a user has searched for in the past. Such information could be sold to advertisers, who could then target users with banner ads or e-mail solicitations related to their *past* searches.

The cookies.txt file already provides a means for doing both of these things. Web servers deposit information (in the form of small text messages called *cookies*) that they have collected about the user from searches or other interactions into the cookies.txt file on the user's PC. The process is as simple as delivering search results to the user's screen, only the information in the cookie is intended for the server (rather than the user) to look at in the future.

So far the cookies.txt file only holds information pertaining to a particular PC. Any user of the PC will add to its cookies.txt file simply by surfing the Web and visiting sites that deposit cookies. Servers usually only identify a user by the IP address attached to communications, which is unique to the PC, but not to the user; however, if the server used other means to identify distinct users more precisely (such as by soliciting an e-mail address or account name) it would be possible to store this information in the cookies.txt file, or even in a database on the server. It would not be too hard to gather such information, either from the client PC or directly from the user.

IMPLICATIONS OF A TOOL'S COMMERCIAL NATURE TO ITS USERS

One of the most obvious implications of competition between Web search tools is that they have little incentive to be forthcoming about their abilities and weaknesses. They also have a negative incentive to refer users to competitors, even when referral could be to the user's benefit. We do not mean to imply that any of the current search tools consciously lie about themselves to their users, nor that it is a necessary consequence of doing business. With few exceptions, though, search tools do a far better job of promoting than of explaining themselves. Help files too frequently contain more hyperbole and sly jabs at rivals than thoughtful instruction. Since so much of the search process is hidden from the user (the harvesting process, the indexing, search algorithms, ranking), it is quite difficult to learn how a particular tool behaves. Further, the Web is too elusive to form a solid basis for comparison. This is one reason we have avoided statistics in our evaluations, in favor of a subjective evaluation from a user's perspective. It is impossible to calculate realistic values of the Web—there is no reliable way to measure it—which makes it tough to evaluate the recall and precision of an individual harvesting robot by objective (or at least numerical) criteria. Web statistics have to be part of the equation, and most sources get their Web statistics from the search tools to begin with. The lack of information offers plenty of opportunity for Web search tools to make untestable claims of their abilities.

All institutions try to protect their own existence, just like individual people. Search tools with stockholders, customers, products, services, and brand names have powerful incentives to continue to exist and to grow, thus creating conflicting interests within the organization. On the one hand, competition and rapid innovation in technology create a desire to focus efforts on research and development, to constantly improve the service. On the other hand, increasing size and the accumulated capital investments in past efforts create inertia and a desire to shift efforts to maximize the return on what has already been done. Not surprisingly, companies try to do both. Search tools' frequent tinkering and tweaking of their interfaces are perfect examples of this synthesis. It is a lot easier and cheaper to add graphics and better designs to the interface than to rebuild the Web index, overhaul the search engine, or develop new harvesting and indexing robots. Cosmetic changes are also far more obvious to the user, who is inclined to judge the tool by the interface too much anyway. An *appearance* of continuous novelty and innovation is a big victory for a Web enterprise of any sort, often bigger than *actual* novelty and innovation. But the real benefit to the user is usually less than other kinds of improvements would provide. Think of it as "virtual improvement."

However they try to accomplish the task, commercial search tools will be persistent in their efforts to survive. University projects are abandoned when key participants graduate or accept new projects and positions. But commercial endeavors accumulate more obligations—to employees, creditors, stockholders, and to themselves as living, growing entities. They will continue to change and evolve in a variety of ways as long as they can. Natural questions of identity thus arise: What about a Web search tool persists over time? What exactly *is* it? If every component is gradually replaced, from the robots to the interface (and the Web itself), what makes WebCrawler continue to be WebCrawler, month after month?

Ontological questions such as these are not just philosophical musings, particularly as search tools desperately cultivate brand loyalty among users. We took notes for a description and evaluation of WebCrawler's interface one day, only to find the interface completely rebuilt a week later. We were forced to revise our description substantially, but more importantly we had to stop and question WebCrawler's identity. What part of WebCrawler had persisted over time, through various stages of development and revision and ownership? What part could we refer to and describe as "WebCrawler" in a manuscript, that would continue to be accurate and relevant in the resulting book, months and many potential changes later? As mentioned earlier, one force operating on commercial search tools is inertia, a tendency to continue moving along the same path. The bigger these organizations become and the longer they exist, the more momentum they build—consequently the force necessary to change their direction increases. Further, this same rule can be applied to the component parts of the search tool. The pieces that embody the greatest investments of resources will be the least likely to change. Although we cannot offer a precise metric by which to calculate the relative worth of each part, it seems obvious that the Web index is the most difficult limb for a search tool to replace. An index covering tens of millions of Web pages, built over years with the most efficient means available at the time, would require a major technological leap to replace it with something better in a short period of time. WebCrawler's index grows by the hour in variety and size, but it uses the same agents and the same formats and processes to do the job. Any change beyond this would almost certainly build on what is already there, limiting the possible deviation in both methods and results. Thus, paradoxically, the index, that part of the search tool that actually changes in size and content with more frequency than any other, represents the most consistent component over time. Search engines and robots can be replaced much more easily, but they cost more to develop and to improve significantly than the interface costs. Thus the interface is definitely the most fluid part of a search tool. This too is somewhat ironic, since a change in the interface is far more noticeable and striking a development from the user's perspective. Interface changes can easily seem like a bigger deal than they are.

Beyond these tangible features, Web search tools have histories, consistent styles, and even personalities that persist as the whole entity changes. All of these factors and qualities are integral to a search tool's identity; however, since they change rapidly in different ways at different times, it is imperative that serious users be conscious of and evaluate each tool with every use. These are very slippery creatures. As soon as you get a grip on one, it slides loose. Just as these tools strongly desire brand loyalty among users, users must consciously avoid it. This is not to say that one tool cannot consistently out-perform others, especially in particular subject areas and types of searches. But it is clear that none will be the best choice for every need. No one tool will index the entire Web any time soon, nor will it ever duplicate its competitor's index or methods precisely. They are likely to eclipse one another as they evolve. Responsible users must continually employ a variety of tools, both for the benefit of individual searches and to provide a means of ongoing evaluation. In a way, each time you use a particular tool, you must evaluate it like a new edition of a reference book. If it is a book you decided to buy in the past, it probably retains some or all of the quality of the previous edition, although it may not. Even if it is just as good as before, there might be a new title or a vastly improved edition of a long-time competitor. The only way to know is to keep looking for alternatives, evaluating and comparing all the time. This is a crucial habit to develop with search tools, particularly as the Web (and online information as a whole) becomes more and more a part of the library and the larger world of information services.

Chapter 14

Yahoo! and Other Prime
Sources of Information

So far we have confined our discussions to a fairly specific model of Web search tools. Recall that each of the tools described in Section III had to be widely recognized and free to the public, use robots to discover and index documents, and harvest all categories of Web pages as it finds them, regardless of subject. These tools provided no pre-coordinated structure for their mammoth collections of pages, such as a classification system or a browsable list. They supply no editorial judgment, nor any conscious collection development. The lack of any one of these three features would have prevented these tools from creating indexes that even begin to approach the full size of the Web.

However, this model by no means describes all of the valuable public collections of pointers to Web documents. We have recommended that readers strive to use multiple search engines to increase the percentage of the Web they search. We also recommend using a variety of other Web tools, especially those providing clear, quick access to handpicked collections. This chapter offers brief looks at several different models, all of which employ human judgment to gather and arrange collections of Web sites and pages. Do not interpret these descriptions as full reviews, since we have not tried to be as comprehensive or critical in examining these tools as in the earlier search engine chapters.

YAHOO!

http://www.yahoo.com

Yahoo! has frequently served as a counterexample in our earlier discussions of Web search tools, since it offers a very different interface and index. Although

Yahoo! does offer a familiar command-line search interface to its database, its outstanding feature is a browsable, hypertext classification structure connecting every item in its collection. Yahoo!'s editorial staff creates subject and form categories (also called *headings*), links these categories together, and gathers Web documents under them. Users may browse the levels of these categories to reach groups of links to Web pages. Just like the search engines, Yahoo! does not actually archive Web pages, nor does it present them to the user. Rather, it creates a surrogate record for each page or site, composed of a brief description, title, and URL, which it displays to users as a link to the actual page on its home server. Unlike the search engines, this is all that Yahoo! indexes from each page. Thus users cannot search any of the actual text of a Web page from the command-line interface. Yahoo! makes up for this by ensuring that its classification headings quickly lead users to collections of appropriate documents.

How Yahoo! Adds Documents to Its Collection

Yahoo! discovers new Web pages primarily by author or publisher submission. Users who wish to submit a new URL must browse Yahoo!'s classification headings until they find what they judge to be the best place for their page to be linked. Once there, the **Add URL** link at the top of the page retrieves a form containing several fields that request information about the new page and the user. Since the user has already identified a preferred heading, the **Category** field form arrives containing that heading by default. Users may suggest two or three other appropriate headings in the **Additional Categories** field, as well as suggest new headings for Yahoo! to add to its classification structure. (Yahoo!'s staff may or may not act on suggested new or additional categories.) The rest of the form offers fields for the URL, title, user's name and e-mail address, and optional geographic information. The **Comments** field provides space to compose a 15- to 20-word description of the page, which users will be able to read and search. Yes/No check-boxes ask if the new page incorporates Java or VRML. A similar **Change** form allows users to update or correct any of this information for pages Yahoo! has already collected, although only the contact person or user who originally submitted a page can request changes in its Yahoo! entry.

Yahoo! does discover a small number of new Web pages by using a robot, but provides no detail as to how this robot behaves. Clearly Yahoo!'s robot is far less important to its performance than is the case for the search engines we have discussed, so users need not feel as cheated by the lack of information.

Classification and Indexing

Whereas automated search engines use software to analyze and index Web pages, Yahoo! relies solely on human judgment (remember, its robot only *discovers* new documents). As we mentioned, users may suggest preferred and additional categories for classifying the pages they submit. Yahoo!'s editorial staff maintains the right to place pages elsewhere within the structure of the collection as needed. Yahoo! also reserves some headings and category levels to which only its staff can add new URLs. These include the top levels of the classification structure, regional headings, the *Government* heading, and others. (Yahoo! maintains a full list of its reserved headings.) Other protocols govern special types of pages. For example, business pages must be linked to a *Business and Economy* heading, with a maximum of two headings total. Personal home pages must be placed under an *Entertainment/People* heading.

Like some of the other tools we have discussed, Yahoo! offers a user interface incorporating several different collections and ways of accessing them. For its search engine, Yahoo! indexes URLs, titles, and comments. Users may perform keyword searches which cover the contents of all three of these fields, but the best way to use Yahoo!'s main collection of Web pages is to navigate the hierarchical classification system of hypertext links.

Interface and Searching

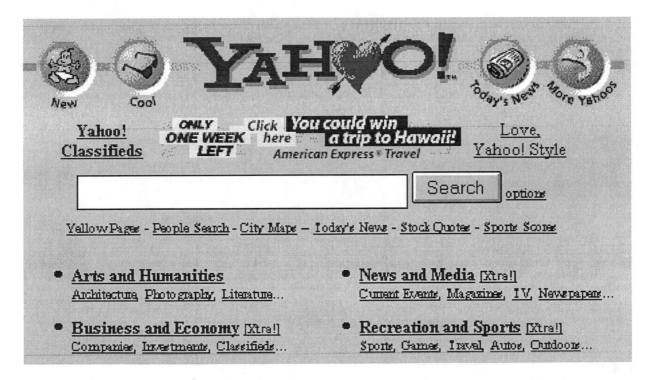

A list of 14 broad subject (for example, *Social Science*) and form (for example, *Regional*) headings dominates Yahoo!'s home page. Each of these primary headings (Yahoo! sometimes refers to them as "meta level categories") is a link to another list of more specific subheadings, which are themselves links to further subheadings and—eventually—lists of links to actual Web pages related to the specific subject. A number following a heading indicates how many links to ac-

tual Web pages are classed under that heading. Although users may have to follow several links to reach a list of pages, the resulting sets frequently produce a
much higher percentage of relevant hits than a typical search in a massive search
engine. For many types of searches (especially when first exploring a new topic
to see what's available) this can save a lot of time, since the user need not en-
gage in much trial and error search revision, nor browse through huge results
sets.

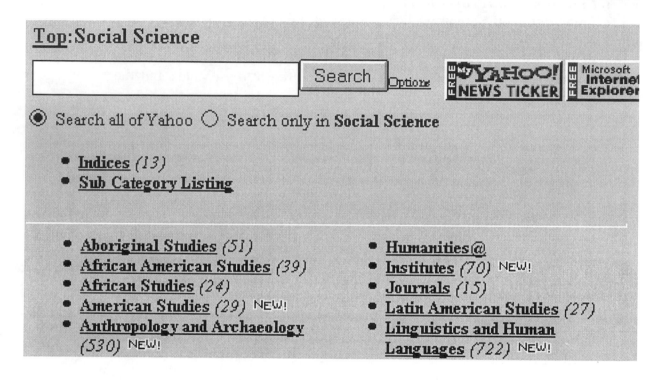

Clicking any of the primary headings on the Yahoo! home page, such as **Social Science**, retrieves a similar list of subheadings. Each of these subheadings
lies one level below the primary heading in the hierarchical structure—in other
words, they all hold equal ranks in the classification system. However, rather than
force the user to continue moving down the hierarchy one level at a time, Yahoo! provides a **Sub Category Listing** link just above the list of subheadings.
This link retrieves a map, in an indented outline format, of the entire hierarchy
of subheadings lying below the primary heading. Although this outline may be
quite long (sometimes several screens worth of downward scrolling), it gives users a chance to see the whole picture of how a broad category is organized within
Yahoo!, as well as a chance to skip a few steps by jumping ahead or sideways in
the classification system.

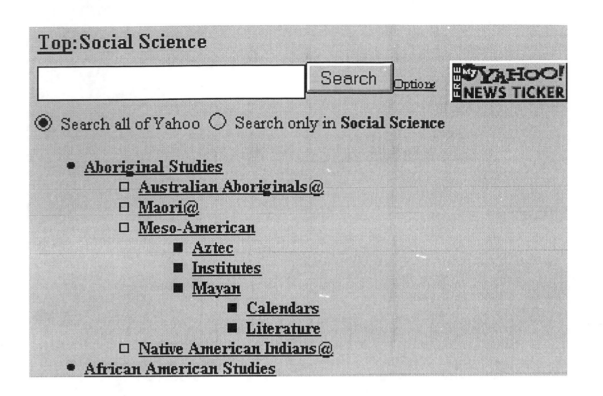

Indices links usually lie just above the ***Sub Category Listing*** link on a page of subheadings. An *Indices* link retrieves a group of links to other sites on the Web that are themselves collections of links and documents pertaining to the current subject. This is sort of like Yahoo! sending the user to other, miniature Yahoo!s devoted to a particular topic. (In fact, this feature mimics one of the primary functions of the Argus Clearinghouse and WWW Virtual Library, discussed below.)

Above the list of primary headings, Yahoo! provides a single command line. Users may type one or more keywords, which Yahoo! automatically searches against its indexes of headings, Web pages, current events, and news items. If a search fails to match any categories or Web pages, Yahoo! automatically searches AltaVista's index of the Web. Users may add the ubiquitous plus (+) and minus (–) sign operators to specify that certain keywords must or must not occur in the results, although parentheses are apparently not available for complex Boolean queries. Quotation marks around multiple keywords search for phrases, and an asterisk (*) at the end of a word enables truncation. Users may restrict a keyword search to the title or URL fields in a Web page record by preceding the keyword with a *t:* or *u:*. However, plus and minus operators must appear to the *left* of these field indicators, not to the right. For example,

is correct, while

is not.

The **Options** link next to the command line takes the user to a different search form with more features, but with little more functionality. On the Options form users can choose—by checking the appropriate box directly below the command line—to search Yahoo!'s indexes (the default on the previous search form), Usenet, or a directory of e-mail addresses. If the user chooses to search Yahoo!'s collection, a second set of check-boxes allows him or her to specify a search of Yahoo!'s categories (the headings themselves), Web pages (titles, URLs, and comments), news articles, or a current Internet events calendar.

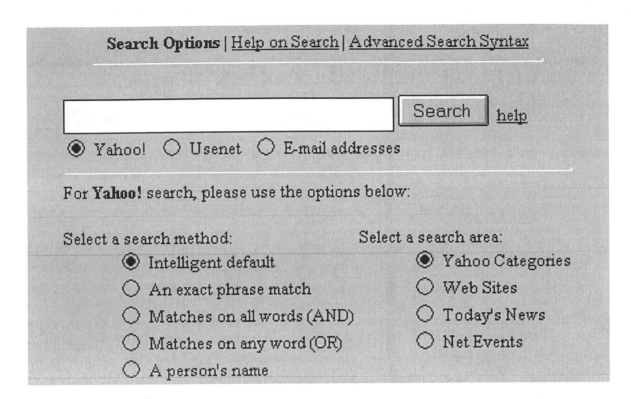

More check-boxes provide choices of search methods, just like those of several of the major search engines: *Intelligent default, An exact phrase match, Matches on all words (AND), Matches on any word (OR),* and *A person's name.* Yahoo! never defines the *Intelligent default* option in any of its Help files or other documentation. It seems to behave like the default option on most Web search engines, which connects all keywords with **OR**, then relies on the ranking process to move the "best" results to the top of the list. The familiar *An exact phrase match, Matches on all words (AND), and Matches on any word (OR)* options serve as shortcuts to using the quotation marks and plus and minus symbols by connecting all the keywords in a query with the corresponding operator. A drop-down menu allows searchers to restrict results to Web pages added to Yahoo! during the last day, three days, week, month, three months, six months, or three years. A second menu restricts results pages to 10, 20, 50, or 100 hits apiece.

As mentioned, when a search fails to match any categories or Web pages, Yahoo! passes (or rather *punts*) the search to AltaVista, which then checks its larger, robot-generated index of Web pages. Yahoo! discards any operators and options the user may have chosen from the check-boxes or menus before sending the search to AltaVista, and when AltaVista sends back the search results, Yahoo! formats them for the user. The end result is that the user never has any direct contact with AltaVista, helping Yahoo! avoid passing off customers as it uses other sites to satisfy a search.

Results and Ranking

Like most search engines, Yahoo! presents keyword search results as a ranked list of links composed of titles and comments; however, since Yahoo! is primarily focused on its classification system, hits in the results are grouped under their common subject headings. Yahoo! mentions three criteria it considers in ranking results: number of keywords associated with the page; fields in which keywords occur (words in the title rank higher than the comment or URL); and category level (broader categories rank above the narrower categories). Since pages are grouped under their common categories, however, it is unclear how Yahoo! reconciles its ranking criteria. Consider two pages that appear next to one another under the same heading in the results of a search. Should the user assume that both of these pages also contain the same combination and number of search keywords? Should the user assume these keywords are also in the same fields in both pages? If not, do these distinctions only matter when ranking these two pages relative to one another within a single category? Yahoo! provides no answers.

Despite this confusion over the ranking process, it is clear that Yahoo! integrates its classification structure into its search results, just as it does in most other facets of the site. Not only do the headings group and classify Web pages in the results, but since the headings are themselves links, they also serve as active members of the results set. Yahoo! does a fine job of weaving its primary asset into all of its services. On the downside, Yahoo!'s visual format for combining headings and Web links produces an inefficient page that gets fewer hits on a screen than the average search engine. Users must scroll a long time to explore large searches.

Summary

Since robots and search engines cannot comprehend or establish semantic links between texts, Yahoo!'s hand-crafted classification system provides a vastly different means of retrieving Web documents. Search engines like AltaVista place the responsibility on the user for establishing links between documents. A given set of search results does not exist until a user creates a search statement composed of semantically related words and submits it for automated comparison to the index. On the other hand, Yahoo! greets the user with a clear, stable structure that already connects every document in its collection to every other. It assures even a clueless user a place to start and a path to follow to the resources in the site. On the flip side, Yahoo! cannot match the range of potential combinations and permutations available from a massive search engine. Flexible keyword searches, especially of full-text databases, offer the chance to coax out any conceivable relationship between texts, provided the user can produce the necessary query. Smart searchers should use both of these complementary organizational schemes to best exploit the wide range of information on the Web.

Having said all that, Yahoo! still does not encompass the rest of the universe of worthwhile Web retrieval tools. In the next section we conclude with a glimpse of several sites that add other value and structure to Web resources.

MAGELLAN

http://www.mckinley.com

Produced by the McKinley Group (a collection of publishers based in California), Magellan is sort of a cross between Yahoo! and Excite, with reviews. It acquires new sites to review from Excite, which gathers new URLs via robots and user submissions. Magellan also employs Excite's search engine software, but like Yahoo!, searching is not Magellan's *forte*. Instead, Magellan concentrates on maintaining a classification structure and providing reviews for most of the sites and pages in its collection.

Pictures reproduced with the permission of Excite, Inc.

Magellan's editors provide useful, subjective reviews (usually about a paragraph long) and numerical rankings for as many pages as they can, working from a queue of new URLs sent by Excite. Editors calculate rankings based on a site's comprehensiveness and currency of content, ease of use, and "net appeal" (which is something like a fun factor). Each site or page receives a score of from one to ten points in each of these three areas, and an overall score found by summing the other three. In addition to these scores and reviews, editors also review sites based on their suitability for children. Magellan rewards sites deemed safe for impressionable minds with a "green light" icon next to their entry. Editors also exclude "objectionable" sites, such as those "that relate to pornography, pedophilia, or hate groups." So far as we know, Magellan is the only tool we discuss that actively censors its index by subject matter. The extent of these guidelines is unclear.

We have already discussed in detail Magellan's process of discovering documents, as well as its search engine interface, in the earlier chapter on Excite. Nevertheless, it is worth mentioning again that Excite's robots are very finicky and ignore several popular document formats (PDF for example) and features (such as HTML meta tags), which can limit Magellan's scope. Magellan's classification structure is adequate, although nowhere nearly as detailed (it only extends two levels deep) or wide-ranging as that of Yahoo!. The added value of quality reviews (unlike some sites, Magellan actually gives unfavorable reviews, at times), however, makes Magellan a useful source to keep in mind.

THE ARGUS CLEARINGHOUSE

The Argus Clearinghouse is a type of meta-tool comprising lists of lists of Web sites and pages. Argus (the company) is composed primarily of professional librarians who choose and evaluate "*guides*," large topical collections of hand-picked links collected and reviewed by independent subject authorities all over the Internet. According to the Clearinghouse's home page, Argus bases its approach on the belief that "for the most part, language and ideas are simply too ambiguous for automated retrieval systems to properly identify and evaluate . . . so intellectual labor is necessary to provide qualitative assessment of the Internet's information." (To which we add a hearty "Amen!") True to this faith, Argus relies entirely on human effort to find and organize Web resources, going so far as to require names, contact information, and biographies of a guide's author(s) to facilitate further resource sharing between producers and users.

The Premier Internet Research Library

What's New | Clearinghouse Information | Credits
Search | Ratings System | Submit a Guide | Guide of the Month

Arts & Entertainment
Business & Employment
Education
Engineering & Technology
Environment
Government & Law
Health & Medicine
Humanities

Used with permission of Argus Associates, Inc.

Argus ranks guides with a metric similar to Magellan's, although more detailed and helpful. Argus requires that the guides it reviews be more than lists of topically related links—authors must describe, evaluate, and organize all of the links they include. Argus rates guides from one to five on each of these three facets, looking for complete site descriptions (covering resources, traffic, intended audience, update frequency, Help files, and so forth), careful subjective evaluations (of content, usability, authority, and reliability), and clear (and preferably *mul-*

tiple) organizational schemes (such as by subject, format, audience, authors). Argus's reviews are quite critical, when necessary.

In addition to laudable content, Argus put the cherry on top by offering the simplest, most accessible interface we have used on the Web. There are no ads, no Java, almost no graphics (only the logo!), and clear links to everything on the site. Argus has a weak search engine, but we rarely find reason to use it. In fact, our only problem with the Argus interface is its *over*-simplified classification system, which offers only one level of categories. True, the guides listed under these categories do serve as subcategories, since they each lead to a wealth of other related links, but their titles are frequently not specific enough to serve as good headings, and the resulting lists of guides can take a while to scroll through. On the whole, though (and *especially* for academic users seeking subject overviews and contact with authors), the Clearinghouse is one of the most rewarding tools on the Web.

THE WWW VIRTUAL LIBRARY

Founded at CERN in 1991 by none other than Tim "Father of the Web" Berners-Lee himself (as a way to keep track of his creation), the WWW Virtual Library Project has since changed hands and moved. Arthur Secret replaced Lee as the director of the Virtual Library at CERN in 1993, then moved the project with him to the World Wide Web Consortium (W3C) in 1996. Like the Argus Clearinghouse, the Virtual Library is a meta-tool, which organizes a list of links to lists of links (say *that* three times fast). Also like Argus, the Virtual Library does not produce topical lists of its own, but instead links its subject headings to authoritative guides produced and maintained by independent authors all over the world. Unlike Argus, the Virtual Library does not provide ratings or rankings of its guides.

From the user's perspective, the Virtual Library is simply one long page of subject headings, a few of which have brief annotations or cross-references. Each heading links to one guide, such that the classification structure is even shallower than that of Argus (which at least groups multiple guides under each of its headings, although it has far fewer headings). The Virtual Library leaves most of the look and content of the underlying guides entirely up to their respective authors, except for a few formatting requirements. It provides no search engine (a third-party engine was recently dismantled) and maintains no other interface to its collection, except for a list of e-mail links to contributors.

Ultimately the WWW Virtual Library is a better idea than it is a reality. Argus provides much the same service with a better interface and a larger collection (which overlaps the Virtual Library, to boot). Even though the Virtual Library offers many superior guides, we have included it here largely because of its historical significance and wide recognition.

Chapter 15

A Last Thought

The Web offers far more search-and-retrieval tools than we have mentioned in this book. In particular, there are myriad sites that concentrate only on specific subjects and disciplines. Most of these follow the models and examples we have discussed (for example the individual guides that make up Argus and the Virtual Library are subject-specific tools in their own rights); others do and will strike out on their own with unique organizational and interface structures. For the most part, though, any tools users are likely to encounter in the near future will resemble one of the models or examples we have provided. The key to using new tools is to develop critical skills and practice, practice, practice. We would *most* like readers to realize that there is not, nor ever will be, a perfect search-and-retrieval tool—on the Web or in any other environment. Never take tools at face value and never rely on just one.

APPENDIXES

Appendix A

Search Engine Features to Evaluate and Describe

Brief History	Creator, Sponsor, Location, Ownership, Purpose/ Philosophy, Size, Rate of growth, Dates, Quotes
Human Effort	To what extent is the process automatic? Are there any human-defined broad categories, or a hierarchy, or cataloged records, or controlled indexing, or a review/screening process?
Updates	How often? How extensive? Is there a fixed amount of information retrieved each time, or is it variable (e.g., gets bigger every time, depends on submissions)?
Interface	How is the interface? Confusing/clear, simple/complex, cumbersome/speedy? Does it offer more than one (e.g., a simple screen and an advanced one)? If so, is the distinction between them clearly presented? Will it accept *any* submitted query and then morph it into a form it accepts, or give the user an error message (and if it does, does it assist in reformulating the queries), or simply a null retrieval set?
Boolean	Is it present? To what extent? Proximity?

Boolean Alternatives	Are there any present (e.g., a classification structure à la Yahoo!)
Help	Are there any help files? Do they help? Do they lie? Do they give the option of human assistance, or some further instruction elsewhere? Is using them slow and prohibitive?
Discovery	Where does the site get its documents? Are they submitted or chosen by people? If automatic, how does the robot decide where to go? What are its short-term and long-term goals (e.g., to get a sample from every server available, then evaluate and decide to go to some for greater depth)? Is there a clear way of presenting this algorithm?
Harvesting	What does it retrieve/index (URLs, descriptions, abstracts, full text)? Does it behave the same at each server? If it varies, how does it decide when/what to index? Does it ever decide *after* the user request to go after new sites, things it has not indexed (e.g., a robot on command)?
Stopwords	What are they? Is there a method set up for adding new ones? Is the mistaken use of a stopword in a search deleterious, and is it distinguishable from using a valid term that exceeds the maximum retrieval limit? Or is that how stopwords are defined for the system to begin with?
Search Terms	Does the engine look for the character strings wherever, (e.g., even when embedded in other words)? Are phrases/multiword terms allowed/effective? Is there case sensitivity? How is punctuation treated? (Can it be searched, is it ignored, does it signal the end or beginnings of "words" in the full text?)
Truncation	Is it available? If so, are there any restrictions (e.g., only x number of characters allowed, only certain characters allowed)? Can you use it anywhere besides the end of the word? If so can you use more than one per term?

Results Sets	Are they ranked? If so, how? Is this explained (clearly)? Can the user choose between methods of ranking/ordering? If so, how? Can the user limit the retrieval beforehand and/or after searching (e.g., by maximum number retrieved, by date)? Is there a maximum retrieval set?
Case Sensitivity	Is there case sensitivity other than what would fit in the above categories?
Special	Are there unique or special/rare features not covered above (e.g., produces sets of random links for launching points)?
Retrievals	How did the engine meet or fail to meet the information needs from which our searches were derived?
Cost	Is there a fee? If so are there limited ways to use it free? What is the fee? Is it worth it (i.e., what makes it superior to the free ones)? How can you pay (before use, after, with credit cards, with blood)? If it is free, will it remain so? Do they accept advertising?

Appendix B

Comparing Search Tools

Search Tool	Best Feature	Worst Feature
Webcrawler	Simple user friendly interface and flexible search options	Slow to update index
Lycos	Presentation of search results	Interface is confusing and limits search options
Infoseek	Index is well maintained and up to date	Advertising and self promotion interfere with its interface and help documentation
Open Text	Interface is very powerful and flexible	Database is perfunctorily gathered and maintained
AltaVista	Advanced search form offers great flexibility	Lacks other searchable databases and directories

Search Tool	Best Feature	Worst Feature
Excite	Presentation of search results	Hidden search processes, so the user cannot control truncation, phrase searching etc.
HotBot	Ranking of search results and comprehensive index	Cumbersome interface

GLOSSARY

Glossary

Agent See *Robot*.

Algorithm A set of rules and procedures for performing a task.

Ant See *Robot*.

Applet A small application (i.e., software program). See also *Java*.

Archie A software tool for searching FTP sites. See the Archie text box in Chapter 2 for more information.

ASCII (*American Standard Code for Information Interchange*) A plain text file format; ASCII files contain only a prescribed set of characters and can be interpreted by most computers.

Boolean logic An algebraic logical system for operating on sets of items, using common operators AND, OR, and NOT. For example, the Boolean query *cats and dogs* creates a set whose members are documents common to both the set of documents containing the word *cats* and the set of documents containing the word *dogs*. See Chapter 5 for a longer discussion of Boolean logic and operators.

Breadth-first indexing A harvesting technique in which a robot methodically harvests each link in a single page before moving on to another page. See Chapter 2 for more information. See also *Depth-first indexing*.

Browser Software on the user's PC (i.e., the client) that communicates with document servers on the Internet and displays documents to the user.

CERN European Laboratory for Particle Physics near Geneva, Switzerland, where the Web was born. CERN continues to create standards and improvements for the Web.

CGI scripts (Common Gateway Interface) A standard programming language for creating small applications that connect external applications with document servers.

Click Choose an item on the screen of a Graphical User Interface (GUI) using a mouse or other pointing device.

Concept searching A retrieval method based on concepts, as opposed to terms. Typically involves mapping a single user search term to a set of synonymous or related terms for broader retrieval; can also describe a user search incorporating multiple terms (usually connected with Boolean OR) to describe a single concept.

Cookies.txt A file on the user's PC's hard drive holding notes deposited by a Web server, describing past interactions between the server and the PC. See the Cookies.txt text box in Chapter 4 for more information.

Database A collection of data organized for retrieval. In the context of Web search tools, a database is a searchable collection of electronic index records. See also *fields*.

Depth-first indexing A harvesting technique in which a robot follows the first link on a page to a second page, the first link on that page to a third page, and so on, until finding a dead end. See Chapter 2 for more information. See also *Breadth-first indexing*.

Document A text file, especially a Web page in HTML format.

Domain The portion of a document's URL used to identify the server on which the document resides. For example, *www.mytest.com* is the domain of the URL *http://www.mytest.com/mypage.htm*.

FAQ (Frequently Asked Questions) A file of information about a site or topic, in the form of questions and answers. FAQs often double as user Help files.

Field A piece of information in a database record or document labeled as one of a class common to most records (e.g., title, author).

Fish See *Robot*.

FTP (File Transfer Protocol) A common protocol for transmitting files saved in any format between different computers over telecommunications channels.

Fuzzy AND A technique of searching an index using a set of keywords connected by Boolean OR, then ranking the results so that documents containing all of the keywords are listed first, followed in order by pages with some, then only one, of the keywords. Excite uses this technique.

Gopher Server-side software that organizes documents by placing them in hierarchical lists by subject; users browse the lists through a text-only *Telnet* connection.

Harvest A robot's process of downloading and indexing documents from the Internet. See also *Depth-first indexing* and *Breadth-first indexing*.

Hit A document retrieved by a search. Traditionally a hit refers to a *relevant* document, but Web search tools tend to use the term to describe any retrieved document, so we have done so for clarity.

HTML (***Hypertext Markup Language***) A simple language composed of standardized code that, when inserted around text in a document, provides instructions for a browser on how to interact with and display the document to the user. HTML is a subset of *SGML*.

HTML Tag An HTML formatting code. For example, **<p>** indicates a new paragraph. See also *HTML* and *Meta tags*.

HTTP (***Hypertext Transfer Protocol***) A Standard that defines how information is transmitted across the Web. See the text box in Chapter 1 for more detail.

Hypertext Text serving a second role (besides symbolizing a concept to the reader) as a live link to another body of text. On the Web, clicking a hypertext link calls up a new document or a new area in the same document for the user to view.

IETF (***Internet Engineering Task Force***) A body of volunteers who diagnose and resolve problems on the Internet, as well as develop and expand Internet protocols.

Interface The part of a search tool with which a user makes direct contact, such as the visible display, forms, hypertext, command lines, advertisements. Also refers to the software that produces these features.

Internet A worldwide network of computers, linked into a whole by the use of common communication protocols and standards.

Intranet A network linking computers in a single organization, with a structure and interface patterned on those of the Internet.

Java A programming language developed and marketed by Sun Microsystems, distinguished by its independence from any single computing platforms. Frequently used to create small applications (or *applets*) that can be embedded in Web documents and executed with the browser on a user's PC.

LAN (*Local Area Network*) A network of computers in a single organization, linked together to share programs and data.

LSI (*Latent Semantic Indexing*) Bellcore's retrieval method, based on statistical comparisons of word occurrences between documents.

Meta tags HTML codes that delimit keywords and descriptions about a document for the benefit of a robot or other indexing tool. Meta tags are not normally displayed to a user viewing a page through a browser; for example the meta tag <*META name="keywords" content="dogs, beagles, pets, training"*> would create the HTML equivalent of a topical heading field containing keywords describing a document on how to train beagles.

Modem (*Modulator/Demodulator*) A device that connects two computers over a telephone line by converting the computers' digital signals to and from analog signals.

Online Generally describes interactions between physically disparate computers that maintain telecommunications connections over periods of time. Working on a stand-alone PC without linking to a second computer is considered *offline*; using a PC in conjunction with a *modem*, *LAN*, or *WAN* to communicate with other machines is considered *online*.

Operators See *Boolean logic*.

Parse Separate a document into its component text for indexing purposes.

Precision The percentage of a set of retrieved documents that is actually relevant to the user's information need. For example, if a search retrieves ten documents, but only four are relevant, the search has 40 percent precision. See also *Recall* and *Relevance*.

Protocol A standardized method of interaction recognized by most participants. For example, communication protocols like HTTP are standard methods for encoding and transmitting information between computers that recognize the protocol.

Query A user search statement, i.e., the request a user types and submits to a search engine. Usually composed of keywords connected by operators, or natural language statements.

Ranking Ordering search results into a list, based on how closely each document matches the user query. Usually based on an *algorithm*.

Recall Of all relevant documents in a database, the percentage that is actually retrieved by a user's query. For example, if a database contains ten relevant documents, and a search retrieves four, the search has 40 percent recall. See also *Precision* and *Relevance*.

Relevance How well a document retrieved by a search actually fits the user's information need; one that fits well is *relevant*. See also *Recall* and *Precision*.

Results set The set of documents (or, more precisely, links *to* documents) a search engine retrieves in response to a user query.

Robot Software that automatically searches document servers and then records its findings in a database or index. Also known as *(intelligent) agent*, *spider*, *ant*, *worm*, *crawler*, and *fish*.

Search engine Software that parses a user *query*, compares it to an index, retrieves documents that the index indicates match the user query, and returns a set of results. See also *Search tool*.

Search statement See *Query*.

Search tool The general term we use to refer to Web sites incorporating robots, indexes, search engines, and user interfaces to provide online retrieval of links to Web documents. Synonymous with the common usage of *search engine*, which we define more specifically.

Semantic Pertaining to meaning. Semantic systems attempt to recognize meaning in text, based on statistical measures and patterns.

Server The computer on which a Web page or tool resides. It receives and responds to requests for information from the user's browser.

SGML (***Standardized General Markup Language***) A language for document markup. *HTML* is a subset of SGML.

Spider See *Robot*.

State Protocols that define how computers communicate at a distance *maintain state* (or *are stateful*) if they involve a continuous flow of information over an open connection (e.g., a telephone call, where both parties are continuously connected throughout the call, even when neither is speaking). This is opposed to *stateless* connections, where both parties communicate with discrete packets of information that may each take a different path, and where no one path connects the two computers during the pauses in communication (e.g., a "conversation" by mail, in which each party sends self-contained packages of information whose paths are independent of one another). HTTP is a stateless protocol, while Telnet is stateful.

Stopwords Words so common in the language of the text (and thus rarely indicative of content) that they are frequently ignored during electronic retrieval and indexing. Common stopwords include articles, prepositions, and numbers.

Syntax Rules governing the use and order of a vocabulary of words or other symbols.

TCP/IP (**Transmission Control Protocol/Internet Protocol**) A specific set of protocols for parsing, encoding, transmitting, and reassembling data between networked computers.

Telnet A terminal emulation communications protocol. See the HTTP/Telnet text box in Chapter 1 for a more detailed description.

Term frequency The number of times a user keyword appears within a given document or set of documents. Synonymous with *term occurrence*.

Truncation The shortening of a word, usually by removing the last few characters, in order to retrieve words with a common root.

URL (**Uniform Resource Locator**) The unique identifier, or address, of a Web page. The common format is *protocol://domain:port/path/page*.html. For example, in the URL ***http://www.mytest.com:100/example/glossary.html***, ***http*** is the protocol, ***www.mytest.com.*** is the domain (i.e., the name of the server), ***100*** is the port, ***example*** is a directory on the server (i.e. the path to the document), and ***glossary.html*** is the document file name.

Usenet A network of servers through which users may post and read messages using the UNIX to UNIX Copy Protocol (UUCP). Usenet messages are grouped by common topics.

Veronica (**Very Easy Rodent Oriented Net-wide Index to Computerized Archives**) An index of Gopher menu entries/document names, searchable from most Gopher sites. See the *Archie* text box in Chapter 2 for a more detailed explanation.

W3 Consortium An industry group dedicated to promoting Web standards and interoperability; similar to IETF.

WAN (**Wide Area Network**) A network of computers in different locations connected over long-distance telecommunications media.

Web page A document in *HTML* format available on an *HTTP* server connected to the Internet.

Webmaster The administrator of a Web site or server.

Weight The value added to or subtracted from the relevancy score a search tool generates for a keyword or document during the ranking process. See also *Relevancy*.

Wildcard A symbol, such as an asterisk or question mark, used for truncating query terms and representing variable character positions within words.

WWW (**World Wide Web**) Also known as Web. A network of servers and PCs that communicate with the TCP/IP and HTTP protocols.

Index

About the Authors

Susan Maze, MLS, is the Reference and Systems Librarian for William Woods University in Fulton, Missouri. Susan has also worked as reference and systems librarian for the Saline County Public Library in Arkansas, as well as a researcher studying the organization of medical and scientific literature in electronic environments.

David Moxley, MLS, is a researcher for the Medical Informatics Group and Dr. Mary Ellen Sievert, Professor in the School of Library and Informational Sciences, both at the University of Missouri–Columbia. David is currently co-authoring a textbook on organization of information with Dr. Lynn Connaway.

Donna Smith, MLS, is an information specialist with CSC Index in Chicago. Prior to earning her MLS from the University of Missouri–Columbia, Donna worked as a computer systems analyst. She has traveled internationally working on clinical supply system redesigns. She has worked as an instructor, support specialist, analyst, and researcher within the library field.